Drummer at Kelaniya Dagoba, Ceylon

Dead Cities and Forgotten Tribes

BY

GORDON COOPER

PHILOSOPHICAL LIBRARY

NEW YORK

Published 1952, by the Philosophical Library Inc.
15 East 40th Street, New York 16, N.Y.

TO

IAN FOWLER

Acknowledgments

Acknowledgment is made to John Murray for kind permission to quote the nine lines of verse from Freya Stark's book *The Southern Gates of Arabia* on pages 121-22, and to Messrs. Longmans Green and Co. Ltd., for the two stanzas by Andrew Lang on page 11.

Also to the following for kind permission to use the photographs of which they hold the copyright:—

Ceylon Government Tourist Bureau; Exclusive News Agency Ltd.; Rev. Edwin W. Smith and Macmillan & Co. Ltd.; Thomas Cook & Son; Dorien Leigh Ltd.; Junius B. Wood Esq., and the National Geographic Magazine; The National Museum, Copenhagen; The Royal Canadian Air Force; John Morris Esq., and William Heinemann Ltd.; Public Relations Department, Southern Rhodesia; Her Majesty's Stationery Office; and Paul Popper, Ltd.

Contents

Introduction

PART FOUR

List of Illustrations

"Into the darkness whence they came
  They passed, their country knoweth none,
They and their gods without a name
  Partake the same oblivion.
Their work they did, their work is done,
  Whose gold, it may be, shone like fire
Above the brows of Solomon,
  And in the House of God's Desire.

The pestilence, the desert spear,
  Smote them; they passed, with none to tell
The names of them who laboured here:
  Stark walls and crumbling crucible,
Straight gates and graves, and ruined well,
  Abide, dumb monuments of old;
We know but that man fought and fell
  Like us, like us, for love of gold."

ANDREW LANG

Introduction

It is not easy for the true traveller to diagnose the causes that combine to form the *wanderlust*. An insatiable desire, amounting almost to a passion, for new experiences is certainly one of the most important—a craving to find out what lies on the other side of the unscaled hill.

Of these unexplored joys and thrills which lure some of us ever on, I think few, if any, offer more delicious anticipation than the prospect of reaching the site of some past civilization. It is in such places that one's historical imagination can call up the most exciting and thrilling visions of what once took place on land which, to the unimaginative, may carry not the slightest message.

This same interest, in another direction, applies to primitive and little-known peoples. It is, indeed, rather astounding in this present world to find so large a number of unique clans and tribes scattered all over the world. Ethnography and archaeology are superb pastimes, and persons who travel without being engrossed in them miss much.

The ancient Egyptians and the Sumerians, who inhabited the area between the rivers Tigris and Euphrates which now forms part of Iraq, share the distinction of having been the first architects. (I know that Professor L. S. B. Leakey claims that a town near Ngaruka in Central Africa was founded about 20,000 years ago, but this is problematical.) The oldest known brickwork, dating from about 3500 B.C., was constructed by the Sumerians, while the oldest building of stone masonry, dating from about 2940 B.C., was erected by the Egyptian architect, Imhotep. This building, the tomb of King Zoser, is usually referred to as the Step Pyramid.

Excavations have been carried out at several ancient centres of Sumerian civilization, and the results achieved have been fascinating. The same can be said of other places all over the world where digging up history has taught us that many ancient civilizations had just as high standards of living and social amenities as we possess to-day.

At Mohenjo-Daro and Harappa are the remains of cities which date from about 3000 B.C. They are the oldest architectural relics yet discovered in India. The building materials used were brick, mud and gypsum mortar.

Because of the extreme antiquity of Chinese civilization one might reasonably expect to find the remains of ancient cities in China, but the majority of the earliest Chinese buildings were constructed of timber, a material which does not usually stand exposure to the elements for more than a few generations. The oldest surviving buildings in China are tombs, since the Chinese, venerating the dead, sought to give them lasting memorials, and made use of stone for this purpose. There is also the Great Wall of China, built before 200 B.C., and perhaps the greatest piece of architectural construction in the world.

Hidden away in Central American jungles are the remains of ancient stone and concrete cities, some of which were built between A.D. 300 and A.D. 500 by a number of Indian tribes who are known under the collective description of Mayas, a term signifying a unity of language but not of race. The Mayas had attained a high level of culture by about A.D. 200, but their civilization began to decline about A.D. 900, and was practically extinct by the time the Spaniards arrived, in the sixteenth century.

The Mayas displayed an extraordinary skill in architecture and sculpture, despite the only tools at their disposal being of stone. They knew nothing of iron and its uses nor of the principle of the wheel, which means that they must have devoted an incredible amount of labour to quarrying, carving and transporting their building materials. The late Roger Fry, the well-known painter and art critic, was of the opinion that the Mayas ". . . working only with Stone Age tools, have left us more masterpieces of pure sculpture than the whole of Mesopotamian, or more than the majority of modern European civilizations."

The Gateway of the Sun, Tiahuanaco, Bolivia

Batwa Village built on a Northern Rhodesian swamp

In South America the ground has barely been scratched as far as unearthing the past life of cities is concerned. We know that peoples of the long past who lived there built great cities showing the highest artistic standards.

While some modern cities—London and Rome are two examples—are built above the sites of former towns, there are other entire cities which have been rebuilt of old materials. Kairouan, the desert city, was built out of the ruins of Carthage, just as present-day Cairo was built out of age-old Memphis. Salerno, near Naples, was built out of some of the ruins of Paestum in the fifth century. The list is, indeed, almost endless.

In the present volume I have not attempted to present what might be termed the most important dead cities. They would be hard to define in any case. Rather have I chosen those special places which have particularly interested me and which in most cases I have myself visited. By making a selection from different parts of the world there is a more varied interest for the reader, who will gather that as an individual I have *felt* the historical atmosphere more strongly in some places than in others.

When it comes to forgotten, or perhaps more correctly termed, unique and primitive tribes, the choice has again had to be personal and selective. In the course of one's wanderings so many unusual peoples are encountered, almost all of whom are worth writing about.

Only recently I was travelling through Sardinia and came upon peasants who still speak Latin and can barely understand the Italian tongue. Again, on the small adjoining island of S. Pietro the inhabitants speak ancient Genoese and are quite different in type and behaviour from the rest of the Sardinians.

Racial fragments, whose relationship to races now flourishing is difficult to discover, and which through in-breeding and a restricted mode of living have become doomed to extinction, are to be found tucked away in holes and corners over all the world. Among them are the dwarf Miaotsze, the original inhabitants of China, the aborigines of Japan, and the Ainu of the northern island of Japan who, with the Chukchis, the Gilyaks, the Yukaghirs and others, form the relics of the ancient Siberians.

The aborigines of India are the dark-skinned Mundas. In one of these tribes, the Ho, matriarchy (the social organization in which the mother, and not the father, is the head of the family, and in which descent and relationships are reckoned through mothers) is still continued, as it is among some other primitive peoples. Ceylon is still the home of the Veddas; on the Andaman Islands, in the Bay of Bengal, are aborigines who have, it is said, not yet learnt the art of making fire, and on the Phillipines are the pygmy Itaves. The original population of Siam is composed of the negrito Semang, another tribe of pygmies.

The average height of most of these aboriginal peoples, of whom the greater part are few in numbers, unique of their kind, and certainly almost "forgotten", ranges between three feet and six feet. The Puri and Barniri in the interior of Brazil, the Batwa in Northern Rhodesia, who are intellectually inferior to all African natives, the Akkas of Central Africa, the Bagielli in the southern Cameroons, and the Hottentots, probably the oldest people in Africa along with the Bushmen, are all small in stature.

In South America there still survive the pygmy tribes of the Makako and the Inje-Inje, whose language consists of a few words. Of the inhabitants of Tierra del Fuego (who have now been moved elsewhere) a mere handful remain; the last Tasmanian woman died in 1876.

As far as ancient European peoples are concerned, the Albanians are the only racially pure relic of the Illyrians who settled in the Balkan peninsula in the Stone Age; while the only pure relic of the Basques, who once as the Iberians (belonging to the Hamitic race, in its turn related to the Semites) inhabited the whole of western Europe, is now to be found ensconced in a corner of the Pyrenees. The name "Basque" means mountain dweller, as does also the name "Albanian". The tiny state of Andorra, which I recently explored, is Basque.

Are there any still undiscovered human tribes? It is probable; for buried in the forests of still unexplored Amazonia are many peoples who have not yet seen a white man. Possibly in central Asia, hidden away in the mountains, there may be relics of some primitive race.

Not so long ago an anthropological expedition from Cape Town University discovered a long-lost tribe, a branch of the Bushmen. Known as the Strandloopers, they certainly existed at the time South Africa was first discovered. They may be termed "Sea-faring Bushmen", for they lived by the sea and their diet consisted almost entirely of seafood. The few remaining specimens of this tribe were discovered living in a cave on the grim and lonely coast of south-west Africa.

I read too, as I write this, of the finding by Lt-Com. Peter Scott of a "new" colony of forty Eskimos called the Kogmuit tribe.

The evacuation or movement of whole populations is no new thing. This has left many pockets of peoples who are quite different from their neighbours. Saracinesco, in the Sabine Mountains, near Rome, was founded in the ninth century by Arabs who still only marry among themselves. Descendants of the Visigoths are living in various recesses of the Pyrenees. The Averser or Avner, the inhabitants of the Avers, an upland valley of the Swiss canton of Grisons, form a German-speaking island amid a population speaking a Romance language. Probably they originated from a garrison of Hohenstaufen soldiers who were left behind to guard the alpine passes at the time of the Roman expeditions.

However, I must curb my pen over this absorbing topic, otherwise this book may end up by being just one long introduction! That would never do. I hope that in the ensuing pages I may inflame some readers' imagination with a desire to explore still further into the world's dead cities and forgotten tribes.

PART ONE

EUROPE and NORTH AMERICA

Europe

I

GREATEST OF GREEK CITIES

For the intelligent traveller Syracuse in Sicily is possibly the most interesting place in the world.

I approached the city for the first time as the sun was setting. The whole country lay bathed in that deep glow which can be produced only by a Sicilian sky; and I confess that I saw the sublime landscape with the deepest emotion. There was an impressive silence over this vast plain of the dead, where once, and perhaps twice, was decided the destiny of the world. Every feature of the landscape seemed to bear the imprint of history, throbbing events which even to-day bring tears to the eyes.

The effect is overwhelming to anyone who was nurtured in the classics, for every feature bears a well-loved name, dearer far and lovelier than anything Roman can ever be. Sicilian though it may be, there is the atmosphere of Greece, the Greek nobility of form and outline, the grey of the Greek olives, the asphodel, the anemone, and the sea.

Yet, this greatest of Greek cities, and possibly the most beautiful of all cities that have ever been built,[1] is to-day not even a ruin; it has utterly passed away under the energy and neglect of man, the endless days of sirocco, the centuries of summers, the countless winters' rain. And time, eater of all things, has consumed even the dust of what was once so great.

But something *does* remain . . . it remains in the mind, in the beloved pages of Herodotus, the truthful pages of Thucydides, and, yes, in the heart—for ever in the heart.

[1] Cicero, who spent many months in Sicily, describes Syracuse as "the largest of Greek cities and the most beautiful of all capitals. For it is both strong of natural position, and striking to behold, from whichever side it is approached, whether by land or sea."

And then there is the Greek Theatre, not built, but hewn out of the living rock in the natural slope of the hill Neapolis, and probably contemporary with the first stone theatre of Greece. It is one of the largest in the world, and Greek drama is still performed there. There are about sixty rows of seats; the top tier is two hundred and fifty yards round; there are nine sections, and eight wide staircases giving access to the audience. All the seats were free in the old days; they are still free (except at actual present-day performances and then the charge is small), but only little green lizards occupied them on the warm spring mornings when I used to sit there, reading and dreaming.

Nowhere else have I felt my sense of historical imagination so keenly stimulated—and others have told me the same thing. And so, as I sat in that Greek Theatre at Syracuse, I could visualize the vast throng tramping the highways leading to this place; the chariots of the rich citizens, with their slave attendants, making wheel ruts which are still deep in the marble road, and they measure exactly the span of the *carettas* of the present day.

In those far-off days a Greek theatre was the parliament house as well as a centre of culture, and when great deeds were hymned by Greek poets, the words, beautiful in themselves, must have been enhanced a hundredfold by the surroundings.

Both harbour and sea lie stretched out as drop-scene on this mighty stage. The rocks of Taormina, the mountains of Hybla, and the snow-capped summit of Etna are also visible as I turn. What one cannot see is any relic of Syracuse at its zenith—mighty Syracuse, the most opulent and powerful of all the Grecian cities—for then temples, gymnasia, and other sumptuous buildings must have made a striking feature in the middle distance.

The tyranny of memory brings other pictures to the mind, pale and dim, but persistent; vague and shadowy forms— ghost forms—seem to glide past and vanish; a slave hurrying with another silken cushion for his master's seat; a spectator bending forward to catch the golden words of Pindar, as if listening to blind Timoleon's voice.

I picture the arrival of Dionysius the tyrant with his train, wearing his beard with burnt ends, for he will not be shaved for fear of razors, and underneath his flowing robes he wears defensive armour. His two young wives are with him, Doris and Aristomache, married on the same day, and a silent court stands obsequiously and uneasy until the great man is seated.

The play is the *Agamemnon*, a tragedy, and only the very young and light-hearted must have been free from the feeling that tragedy was always near.

The most impressive scene of all was when the old men and women of Syracuse sat in the seats of this theatre to watch something which was unrehearsed, and took place not on the marble stage, but with the setting of the sea beyond. It was the dramatic reality of the last sea-fight against the Athenians that they witnessed.

They had a full view of the bay and the city on the island of Ortygia, and when the curtain was rung down that day the play of Athenian glory in Sicily was done.

Then, the visions pass: there is nothing left to me but the blocks of marble, ruined steps, fallen buildings, broken tombs, empty long ago.

How crude in contrast is the nearby Roman amphitheatre of later construction when, under Augustus, Syracuse was re-populated by a Roman colony. How else, in fact, could there be such a building for the Greeks were unacquainted with such barbarous amusements as combats between gladiators and animals. The place is complete with a centre tank in which the crocodiles were kept, gorged with the bodies of Christians and others after the wild beasts had finished with them. It is a huge enclosure, larger than the amphitheatre at Verona or Pompeii.

You can still wander through the Street of the Tombs. Here are hundreds of square openings where tablets once commemorated the names and attributes of the dead. They have, however, long since been removed. Descending this street of the dead, one comes to the Latomia del Paradiso, a great limestone quarry, looking as grim as its history, though the large square pit is now grown over with lemon trees, olives, and a tangle of ivy and bougainvilleas. Here a winding labyrinth possesses strange acoustic properties—a kind of ancient loud-speaker. A whisper comes back magnified a hundred times, a shout is deafening. It is aptly called the Ear of Dionysius, for it is said that this tyrant used to lodge those he suspected of scheming against him in the dungeon below, while he used to apply himself to the funnel that magnified sound and by that means overhear everything that was even whispered.

There is yet another quarry, the Latomia del Cappuccini—the most tragic spot in all the world. For here it was that the sole survivors of that greatest of all Greek armies, so brilliantly described in the pages of Thucydides (Book VIII, LXXXVI–LXXXVII), were imprisoned. "The Gethsemane of a nation" this Latomia has been called; it is in the garden of the Villa Politi, in Achradina, under the Cappuccini convent, and is by far the largest and most important of all these mighty stone quarries.

Written of by Thucydides, four hundred years before Christ, as then being so ancient that its origin is forgotten:

> It is cut out of rock, excavated to a marvellous depth, and carved out by the labour of great multitudes of men. Nothing can be either made or imagined so closed against all escape, so hedged in on all sides, so safe for keeping prisoners in. Into these quarries men are commanded to be brought, even from other cities in Sicily, if they are commanded by the public authorities to be kept in custody.

The moon had risen as I descended into this Gethsemane. Before me, in my imagination, stood the ghosts of those seven thousand Athenians who had returned to people the scenes of their sufferings. In the bright light of the moon the shrubs, creepers, and flowers faded away and I was left with nothing but the pitiless bare rocks and the steel-blue sky with its burning sun. Bearded war veterans, the splendid youths whom Praxiteles loved to model, staggered about over the bodies of their dead comrades. All were delirious with thirst, many too weak to rise.

Nearby was the figure of one young man who stood reciting passages from Euripides to a small group of fellow-

Ear of Dionysius, Syracuse, from which "a whisper comes back magnified a hundred times"

Greek Theatre, Syracuse, hewn from the rock of the Neapolis

Latomia del Paradiso, once a great limestone quarry

An altar on the island of Ponape, Caroline Islands

sufferers. For the moment they seemed to forget their sufferings, as the low musical voice of the reciter spoke the immortal verse. Were they dreaming for a moment of that distant homeland which none were ever to see again? Of cool glades and babbling fountains? Here was one youth—a mere boy—reclining, evidently worn out by privation and disease, and his eyes seemed to hang upon the reciter's words. Then his head started to droop lower and lower. As his eyes closed he sighed and sank to the ground. His friend, the reciter, stopped to go to his help, bending over him, calling his name. But another weary spirit had flown away from this earthly prison on the wings of divine poetry, leaving only an inanimate body, a smile on its upturned face.

* * *

I would not wish you to think, however, that all the memories of ancient Syracuse are grim. There is, for instance, the Fountain of Arethusa that Shelley loved and sang. It used to be part of the water supply of the ancient city but now it is brackish, for the submarine stream into which the nymph Arethusa, when pursued by the river-god Alpheus, was changed by Diana, turned salt owing to an earthquake. Papyrus plants are growing in the basin. It is a memory rather than a fountain.

The perfect features of the lovely Arethusa have, however, come down to us on what are considered by experts to be the finest coins in the world, engraved by Evaenetus and Cimon—for the great Sicilian coins bear the name of the engraver, so that connoisseurs are often more sure of the masterpieces of coin engravers than of the works of great sculptors. Struck by the Syracusans after their conquest of the Athenians in 413 B.C., they bear on one side the glorious head of the Maid in high relief, and on the reverse a galloping four-horse chariot. These coins were recently on exhibition in London, and can still be seen in the excellent museum at Syracuse. In this museum is also the world-famous Landolina Venus, perfect in figure, but headless.

In Syracuse you live a curious Jekyll-and-Hyde life. One moment you are in the ancient and even mythological past, another in the quite fascinating present. For modern life in the city is not without its interests. Yet always the thought comes back to you of what might have happened to our world if only the Greeks had not indulged in their foolish, internecine wars. Our human race cannot give up its wars, however, and we of the present certainly have nothing to say to the foolish races of the past. Having their example and their fate before us, we are not only foolish but criminal. Some junker of an Alcibiades always arises and demands war, and sheeplike nations "mostly fools", with the slumbering savage and the animal roused in their bosoms, vote him power and acclaim. Then there is war, horror, defeat for some; and thousands of prisoners, like the seven thousand Athenians in the quarries of Syracuse, rot and die for the glory thereof—for the glory! Only to-day none of them get released for reciting Homer or Euripides prettily, as some of those hapless Greeks were released.

It is said that there are stories in stones; but in the barren plateau that was once Syracuse, where all that is left is a meagre pasture for goats and sheep, where the asphodel and the olive alone are at home, it is here that one thinks. It is here, indeed, that one can ponder most, and discover a philosophy in the very dust.

SHEPHERDS OF THE HILLS

*A*mong the high mountains on the borders of Greece and Albania live the most primitive and little-known people in Europe, the Sarakatchans. The name of these mysterious nomads must be unfamiliar to many English people, for little was known of them prior to 1930. The Sarakatchans are true nomads, for they own no land, have no fixed settlements, and live entirely on the produce of their herds of sheep and goats. Even the Lapps who dwell in the Arctic wilderness of northern Europe are more civilized. The Sarakatchans have few contacts with the outside world, for their lives are those of restless shepherds, ever wandering over hill and plain, "hardy mountaineers, nowhere fixed, but always to be found where the wolves have dens and the eagles nests", as David Urquhart described them.

These curious people are to be found wandering in summer among the summits of the Pindus Mountains, but in winter they descend to the plains of Macedonia and Thessaly. Though there are only a few thousands of them, they are divided into two races, the Sarakatchans proper who speak Greek, and the Albano-Vlachs, who speak Vlach, a dialect of the western Balkans. The word Vlach comes from a German root meaning "foreign" and is more familiar to English ears in its everyday forms of "Wales" and "Welsh".

The history of the race is interesting, for the Sarakatchans have not always been nomads. In fact, they have only been a wandering race for a century or so. Before that they lived an ordinary settled existence in the Missolonghi district, but during the Greek Revolution of last century they took to the hills, and have led a pastoral existence ever since. Once again we have an example of the fact that a race can progress from civilization to barbarism, instead of the other way about.

The Vlachs, on the other hand, appear always to have been nomadic, and have been steadily moving southward from the Danube Valley ever since Roman times.

In appearance the Sarakatchans are a tall, wiry race, strong and tireless, as are most mountain people. The Greek-speaking clans welcome strangers with the traditional courtesy of their ancestors, though even nowadays the women are likely to run away and hide at the sight of uninvited visitors. Though most of the men dress in white woollen trousers, and black sleeveless tunics, some still wear the white Balkan kilt called the *fustanella*. From their wide leather belts, trimmed with silver, are suspended small satchels and knives, and each man usually carries a shepherd's staff. The long dresses worn by the women reach almost to the ankles, held in place by a wide girdle about the middle. The contemporary fashion in hats is a curious cardboard affair, looking like an inverted bucket trimmed with silver bands.

The Sarakatchans are organized in small communities under the leadership of a head shepherd known as a *tcherlingas*. The commands of this master-shepherd are law in the nomad community. He it is who arranges the route of the annual migration, for though they own no land the Sarakatchans are compelled to pay rent for the pasturage they traverse. These communities are organized on a basis of voluntary partnership. A number of shepherds will meet together and agree to obey the leadership of a certain *tcherlingas*, and accompany him with their flocks and herds for a period of twelve months. At the end of that time the partnership is either renewed or dissolved.

The arrangements for these voluntary partnerships usually take place in the autumn, at a fair such as that held at Konitz, in the Epirus district of Greece. The master-shepherd interviews various families, and arranges the number of sheep and goats which each will bring. As he is responsible for renting the pasturage, each shepherd must in turn pay him a fee for the pasturage his flocks will occupy. When the fair is over the families separate and do not meet again until the following spring, when they will assemble for the annual migration. Although none of the parties concerned can read or write, a man's word is accepted as sufficient guarantee of his integrity; it is very rarely broken.

The Sarakatchans build themselves huts of reeds, rye-straw or young beech trees, for use as both summer or winter quarters. Their only fixed settlement is the summer village of Mejideh, on the frontier between Greece and Albania (which itself may have been destroyed during the desultory warfare of the past three years). The huts look very much like overgrown beehives, being circular in shape with conical roofs.

To make a beech hut eighty young beeches are needed. Forty are planted in a rough circle, and the rest are tied together at the tops. Branches of trees are then interwoven, until both frameworks are covered. A stout post is then thrust underneath the second lot which is tied together at the top, and it is pushed upward till it just covers the circle planted in the ground. The two sets of beech poles are then lashed together with withies, and the hut is complete. A hole is left in one side to act as a door.

Circular huts have been found most satisfactory, for they keep out the wind and rain better, and are easier to make. But they share this disadvantage with a bell tent, that only a certain number of people can sleep inside them, and as all the members of a Sarakatchan family like to sleep under the same roof, they have had to devise a larger type of dwelling. This has caused them to experiment with oblong huts, which are not so satisfactory, for these require a ridge-pole balanced on two forked posts, which are apt to collapse. Such a "house" only stands about eight feet high. There is little in the way of furniture or equipment inside one of these huts. The floor is of earth, which the occupants sit upon in the day time and sleep upon at night, for there are neither chairs nor bedsteads. A primitive loom upon which the women weave their homespun materials, a few cooking pots, and a number of brass and copper sheep and goat bells, comprise the nomad's scanty possessions.

The Sarakatchans can be truly said to live "the simple life". Their food is cheese and maize bread, milk, and an occasional meal of sinewy meat when one of the flock dies. They are nearly self-supporting, their only luxuries being salt, tobacco, coffee and sugar. They use chips of resinous wood as lamps, and do not need matches, using flint and tinder to light their fires.

Both men and women have their own special tasks, but most of the harder work is done by the women. The men tend the flocks and herds, taking them from one pasturage to another, in the traditional Biblical style. They also milk the animals and make the hard, sour cheese of which the Sarakatchans are fond. Though they have dogs to assist them the shepherds use them only for driving off wolves; the dogs are not trained to assist their masters in rounding-up the sheep.

The women do all the remaining work, from building the beech huts to weaving cloth. Incidentally, weaving presented them with a problem, for as the looms are horizontal the operator has to sit in front as if at a table. But there are no chairs in a Sarakatchan hut, or anything else to sit on; how then could they weave? History cannot tell us what unknown genius solved the problem very simply by digging a hole in the floor of the hut and placing the loom in it. A woman weaver could thus sit on the edge of the hole, with her feet tucked under her and the loom in front.

As the wool which they use is very greasy, the summer settlements have to be pitched near a permanent supply of water in which the wool can be washed. Spinning and weaving the wool takes place during the summer months; in the winter the women knit it into vests, pants and socks. Skirts, shirts and trousers are also made. Nomad women always appear busy, even spinning as they go to get water from the spring, with wooden barrels strapped to their backs.

A few remarks concerning the bells prized by the nomads will perhaps be of interest. Made of copper or brass, the tinkling of these bells can often be heard emanating from a Sarakatchan settlement on a summer evening. A community will usually possess a series of a dozen bells, some tall and thin, others broad and round, graduated from low *doh* to high *me*. Sometimes a celebration will be held, and a dozen shepherd boys, each holding a bell in his hand, will play a tune. Sometimes the master-shepherd himself will play on the bells, strange delicate music like something from a far-off elfland.

There are many other curious things one could write about this little-known pastoral race of south-eastern Europe. The investigation of their mode of living by Mrs. Margaret Hasluck, less than twenty years ago, represented the most serious exploration that could have been done in modern Europe outside of Russia or the Arctic zone. What, for instance, of their strange beliefs? That lightning is the weapon which God has just hurled at the Devil, that the arrival of triplets in a family means that God has cursed them, that the dog would have been ruler of the animals if it had not been for the carelessness of the cat. Even their custom of milking goats from the back, instead of from the side, strikes the Englishman as odd.

One wonders how these people have fared during the ten years of war and civil strife which have made life difficult for the dwellers along the borderlands which fringe the Greek-Albanian frontier. Do they still live in their primitive huts of beech branches? And does the shepherd, after a night on a bed of bracken, still don his sheepskin clothes as dawn breaks, call his dogs, and guide his flocks to the day's pasture-ground? Or have they gone the way of other primitive people who have found themselves engulfed in the complications of warring ideologies? Who can tell?

North America

I

COLONIES OF THE VIKINGS

$\mathcal{W}$hat does the name "Greenland" suggest to you?

A huge island somewhere up near the North Pole covered with eternal ice and snow, the home of a few Eskimos who hunt seals and live on blubber? I think that this is the usual picture which the name conjures up in our minds, for many of us gained our impressions of the country from the well-known hymn which begins "From Greenland's icy mountains, from India's coral strand." Many will probably be surprised to learn, therefore, that far from being an almost-uninhabited icy desert, as long as a thousand years ago Greenland was a flourishing country, a self-governing republic, with a population of several thousand people who made their living by farming and hunting, and trading with Europe and America. But so it was!

Five hundred years before Columbus discovered America Greenland had its own parliament. Then the fertile countryside was dotted with houses and farms, churches and monasteries, and there was even a cathedral with a bishop to administer the diocese of Greenland. For nearly five centuries Greenland was an outpost of civilization, then, for reasons which are unrecorded in history, the population vanished, leaving behind them only the ruins of their homes, farms and churches. You can visit those ruins to-day and, looking at them, ponder over the fate which befell their builders, for the disappearance of the Greenland settlements is one of the strangest episodes in history.

But first let us clear up one or two misconceptions about Greenland. Firstly, it is an Arctic land, but its southern portion is on a level with the Shetland Islands, just north of

Scotland, so obviously all the country cannot be frozen solid all the year round. A glance at the map will show the reason for this anomaly. Greenland is the largest island in the world after Australia—indeed, it is a debatable point whether it is the largest of islands or the smallest of continents—and with its length of sixteen hundred miles it stretches across more than twenty degrees of latitude. Secondly, though a peculiar feature of the island is the great mass of the inland ice—a remnant of the last Ice Age—yet fifteen per cent of the island remains free of ice, an area more than equal in size to the whole of Great Britain.

As a result, the coastal fringes along the southern portion of Greenland have an appearance more temperate than Arctic. One finds winding, green valleys whose rolling hillsides are covered with grasses, sedges and bushes, where willow and birch trees grow to a height of thirty feet. In the spring and summer, when the weather can be quite hot, the landscape is colourful with wild flowers and numerous butterflies flit about; indeed, more than four hundred and fifty species of flowering plants have been found on Greenland. Around the modern Danish settlements one sees cultivated meadows where hay is being dried, little fields of potatoes, cabbages and turnips. Sheep and cattle graze in the pastures.

In 1261 Greenland became a colony of Norway. Since the early eighteenth century Greenland has belonged to Denmark, whose policy has been to protect the seventeen thousand Eskimo inhabitants from exploitation by the white race. The country is kept "closed" to all foreigners except a number of Danes holding administrative positions. All trade is conducted by a department of the Danish Government, which provides the Eskimos with part of their food, equipment, medical supplies and other necessities. The idea is not to let them become too dependent upon the white man's food and luxuries. Owing to the strict medical supervision the Danes have managed to keep the Eskimo free from the various diseases to which the white race is subject, so that their numbers are steadily increasing.

The south-western corner of Greenland is deeply indented

C

by a number of long, winding fjords. Wherever one goes along these fjords the shores contain the remains of old farmhouses and other buildings, showing that at one time this country must have been extensively populated. Foreign scientists, writers and artists are occasionally granted permission by the Greenland Administration in Copenhagen to visit the country. In an attempt to solve the mystery of the disappearance of the old Norse colonies, archaeologists have excavated numerous old settlement sites, and the objects which they have discovered have enabled us to build up a fairly comprehensive picture of life in the vanished settlements.

At Igoliko, near Julianehaab, are the ruins of the cathedral church of St. Nicholas, where in 1126 the Norse colonists founded the seat of their bishop, and, after the Icelandic custom, held their annual parliament. This, the ancient "Gardar", is the largest ruin in Greenland. At Kakortok is the "White Church", the best-preserved Norse ruin in Greenland, which was probably built in the late twelfth century. Numerous houses, stables and barns have been excavated, built of stone quarried on the spot, the walls built without mortar, or with a layer of turf between. The houses were small, owing to the lack of timber for fuel and building. Cattle-byres which were excavated showed as many as a hundred and four stalls for beasts. That the chief occupations of the inhabitants were cattle-breeding and hunting were shown by the great numbers of bones in the kitchen middens, which often stood a yard in height above the ruins of the houses.

Now what of the people who built these places, and who vanished without trace? To attempt some solution of this problem we must consider a little-known episode of northern history, the voyages of the Vikings to the Arctic and to America.

It was Eric Thorvaldsson—popularly known as Erik the Red because of his fiery red hair—who founded the first white colony on Greenland. An aggressive, hot-tempered individual, he was living as a petty chieftain in north-western Iceland when he was outlawed for three years for

murdering a neighbour. A few years previously a Norwegian named Gunnbjørn, whose ship had been driven far
westward in a storm, had reported the existence of an unknown land. Erik the Red decided to spend the years of his
exile in locating and exploring this unknown land.

Accompanied by his family and slaves Erik sailed westward about 982 and reached Greenland. They rounded Cape
Farewell and landed in what is now the Julianehaab District.
Here they spent the winter, while exploring the coasts to
the north. Erik liked the land, and decided that when his
period of outlawry was over he would return to Iceland
and persuade his fellow-countrymen to return with him to
the new country. According to the saga from which these
details are taken, he named it "Green Land" in order to
make it sound attractive to the new settlers, though the
green appearance of the countryside may have been another
reason.

Erik's propaganda was so effective that in 986 no less than
twenty-five ships laden with Vikings, their families and
farm animals, set sail for Greenland. Some of them were
lost in storms, others turned back, but fourteen ships reached
Greenland. Nearly four hundred settlers, their horses, cattle,
sheep and pigs were put ashore. Houses were built, farms
marked out, and the first winter passed without loss of life.

So the new colony began, with new settlers arriving each
year, until at one time the population was estimated at nine
thousand people. They made their living chiefly by cattle-
rearing, hunting and fishing. In 990 the first Greenland parliament was established, this Viking republic being the first
democracy in the New World. Ten years later Greenland
adopted the Christian religion, and continued to be administered by a series of bishops until 1540. The last bishop
who lived in Greenland died in 1377. The later ones did
not go there. So the records of the Roman Catholic church,
as well as the Icelandic sagas, are sources of Greenland
history.

About the year 1000 Leif the Lucky, son of Erik, on his
way home to Greenland from Norway, missed his way and
sailed on until he reached a strange new country. We know

now that this was North America, but Leif Ericsson named the land Vinland or Wineland because of the berries he found growing there. When news of his discovery reached Greenland, various expeditions were fitted out to colonize the new land but these settlements were destroyed by warfare with the Indians. That the Vikings discovered America nearly five centuries before Columbus, historians no longer dispute; they dispute merely as to how far south the people of Greenland actually reached.

Some idea of conditions in Greenland at the height of its prosperity can be gained from the reports of two brothers, Nicolo and Antonio Zeno, of Venice, who visited the country in the latter part of the fourteenth century. Greenland was then divided into two districts, the Eastern Settlement and the Western Settlement, both on the south-west coast; the first corresponded roughly with the present-day Julianehaab District, the latter with the present Godthaab District. The Venetians reported that between them the two districts contained two hundred and eighty farms, two townships with a cathedral, fifteen churches and three monasteries.

The ruins of the Benedictine monastery dedicated to St. Thomas have been uncovered at a place called by the Eskimo Unartok, "The Place where there are Hot-Springs"; the brothers reported that its cells were heated by a warm spring in which the monks also cooked their meals. Other relics of this period which have been excavated were runic stones and bronze church bells, while at Ikigait, "The Place Destroyed by Fire", were found wooden crosses and bodies clad in medieval garments, preserved in the frozen ground of the cemeteries.

That the Greenlanders covered vast distances on their exploring and hunting trips is shown by the discovery at an island near Upernivik, four hundred and fifty miles north of the Arctic Circle, of a stone bearing a runic inscription which reads: "Erling Sigvatsson and Bjarne Thordsson and Enridi Oddsson on the Saturday before Gangdag (April 24) made this". From the style of the runes experts date the inscription at about the year 1330. The hunters were seeking seals, walrus and Polar bears, for the church records show that tithes were paid in seal oil, skins, hides, wool and cloth. Voyages also appear to have been made to the American mainland for timber.

For several centuries regular communication was maintained between Greenland and Europe, via Norway, but in the early fifteenth century these trade relations appear to have come to an end. What happened to the inhabitants of the two settlements after that is only conjecture, though among unexamined papers at the Vatican there may yet be records relating to the last days of the Greenland colonists.

In a letter dated 1448, to the bishops of Iceland, Pope Nicholas V deplores the misfortunes which have befallen the people of Greenland, many of whom had been killed and their homes destroyed by the attacks of barbarians some years previously. In another letter, written forty-four years later by Pope Alexander VI, he mentions that there had not been a resident priest on Greenland for nearly eighty years and that Christianity had almost died out. But as regards what actually happened after that, history remains silent.

Though for three centuries, from 1410 to 1721, the fate of the Greenland settlements remained unknown, they were not wholly forgotten, and God-fearing men in Norway and elsewhere felt a desire to re-establish Christianity in that far-off land. Among them was Hans Egede, a Norwegian missionary, who sailed to Greenland in 1721 and established a new settlement. But though he found the remains of churches and houses and farms, of the people who had built them there was no sign; the only inhabitants of the deserted countryside were fur-clad Eskimos who knew nothing of white men or their religion.

What, then, had happened to some nine thousand Norsemen, who had maintained a civilized way of life in Greenland?

Egede and his successors built up a plausible theory; that for some reason ice-fields began to accumulate off southwestern Greenland so that it became more and more difficult for ships from Norway to reach the colonies, that the Greenlanders became weakened owing to the lack of proper food and iron tools and weapons, which hitherto had been brought from Norway by sailing-ships, and that finally the Eastern and Western Settlements were completely destroyed by attacks of hostile Eskimos, attacks which, in their weakened condition the white people were unable to ward off. It was also suggested that the Black Death was carried to Greenland in the mid-fourteenth century and killed off many of the inhabitants. The exponents of this theory conceded that this final breakdown of civilization in Greenland may not have taken place until thirty years or so after Columbus had discovered America.

Although this theory of the disappearance of the two Norse settlements became the generally accepted one, it was not long before various authorities (the late Dr. Nansen among them) pointed out certain fallacies. It was absurd, for example, to imagine that if the Black Death had reached Greenland it would kill off only the white people and leave the Eskimo unharmed; the reverse, rather, would have been the case. The Eskimo, possessing less resistance to the white man's diseases, would have probably been almost completely destroyed.

Then again, various Arctic explorers denied that the Eskimos would have attacked the Norse settlements; the Eskimos are a friendly race, and would have been much more likely to be helpful and sympathetic toward the white men. As the supply ships from Norway no longer arrived with food and equipment, it was much more likely that the adaptable Norsemen enlisted the help of the Eskimos in hunting for seals, bears and walrus with which the country abounded. For here another fallacy arose; that if the ice did drift further south along the coast, then there would be more, not *less* food, for the best big-game hunting is on the ice floes. It is true that the change in climate which resulted might have put an end to cattle-rearing and the cultivation of crops, but as compensation there would be more to be obtained by hunting.

It seems logical to suppose that as making a livelihood by farming became more and more difficult, the Norsemen became more and more dependent upon hunting. People who live by hunting have to be continually on the move, and the inscribed stone found near Upernivik demonstrates that they were already accustomed to covering great distances. Soon there would be no point in remaining at the settlements, for the best hunting-grounds lay far to the north, and it would be simpler to live in skin tents or in snow-huts in the winter. So the deserted settlements would be left to fall into ruins. The people of the Western Settlement may have already lapsed into a nomadic form of life as hunters, while the people of the Eastern Settlement struggled to keep their farms going.

The view generally accepted now is that the Norsemen disappeared, not by being killed off in warfare, but that as communications with Europe declined they gradually adopted the Eskimo way of life. They intermarried with the Eskimos, and because the Eskimo culture was better adapted for survival in Greenland conditions, the white man's culture gradually disappeared. Within a few generations there would arise a new mixed race of Norse-Eskimo blood, whose only knowledge of their civilized forbears would be a few dim legends and traditions.

This question as to whether the Norse colonies disappeared through extermination or by amalgamation with the Eskimos has split the world of anthropology into two camps. Yet it cannot be denied that a great many of the Eskimos living in Greenland to-day have European blood in them, and when dressed in white man's fashion there is little to distinguish them. It would seem as if they are the true blood descendants of the Eskimo hunters and Norse farmers who lived in Greenland so many centuries ago.

CANADA'S LOST WORLD

One of the most mysterious places in all Canada is the remote, little-known valley of the Nahanni River, in the North-West Territories, where for nearly half a century men have been risking their lives in a vain search for a lost gold-mine. As I write this I have before me a paper containing the names of fourteen people who have gone into that valley and have not returned alive. It has always been known as a place of dread, of fearsome dangers, and all sorts of strange stories and legends have circulated about the valley and the primitive Indian tribesmen who live there.

It is difficult to believe that there should exist in such a modern, civilized country as Canada, in this twentieth century, a region concerning which we have so few actual facts, only legend and speculation. It was said that the Indians were hostile to white men, and I remember, as a boy, talking with men who, trying to penetrate the valley in a canoe, were met by a flight of arrows and forced to turn back. It was said to be a semi-tropical country in the Arctic wilderness, warmed by hot springs and geysers. It was said to be haunted by fearsome beasts, remnants of monsters of prehistoric times. It was said . . .

From earliest times, explorers in the Canadian west had heard stories of a wonderful "tropical" valley hidden among the mountains of the northern wilderness. A valley of great trees and rich green vegetation, where the streams never froze and strange beasts roamed undisturbed by the passing of the ages. From time to time reports were published that the valley had been found. Shortly after the First World War an American survey plane, piloted by a Colonel Williams, was flying across unfamiliar country in foggy weather. The landscape below them was just snow-topped peaks, bare plains and mossy valleys.

The Valley of the Nahanni River, North-West Territories, Canada

Old Norse homestead, Greenland

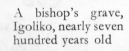

A bishop's grave,
Igoliko, nearly seven
hundred years old

The Castillo and Temple of Warriors, Chi-chen Itza, Mexico

A Jivaro Indian with his blow gun

The shrunken head of a Jivaro Indian's enemy

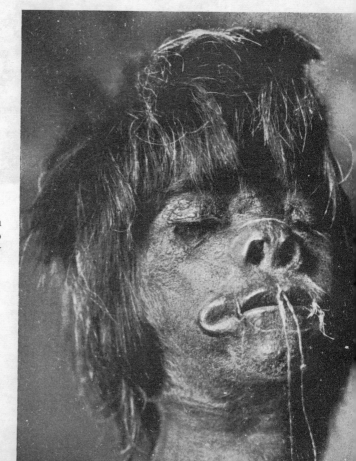

Suddenly they saw a wide valley, thick woodlands and a broad winding stream, above which rose columns of steam. Then the mist closed in again, the valley was blotted out from sight and was seen no more.

The Canadian west had ever been a fruitful source of fantastic stories, but as many of these stories were eventually proved to be true, men began to consider this matter of a "tropical valley" more seriously. The bones of prehistoric beasts were found in the Alberta "badlands", including the almost complete skeleton of a dinosaur; an actual "burning mountain" was found near the Mackenzie River; the existence of a race of giant troglodytes was reported in British Columbia. So the trappers, traders, prospectors and scientists who had hitherto scoffed at the story now wondered if perhaps, after all, there was not something in the tales told by the Nahanni tribesmen of a weird, haunted valley among the sub-Arctic Mackenzie Mountains.

Only the most modern maps of Canada show the South Nahanni River, which rises near the 8,500 foot Keele Peak and flows for three hundred miles through the south-western corner of Mackenzie Territory before it joins the Liard River a hundred miles above Fort Simpson. It flows through a country of thick forests and high mountains, of winding rivers and desolate swamps, the only population being a few hundred primitive Indian tribesmen. Not many of them had ever entered the upper valley, for they believed the place to be inhabited by a race of head-hunters who killed and ate anyone who fell into their hands.

That there was something malignant about the valley was shown by the number of tragedies which took place there. In 1904 William and Frank MacLeod, sons of the Hudson's Bay Company's factor at Fort Simpson, started up the river to look for gold. They were dour, hard-headed Scotsmen who scoffed at the Indian tales of the dangers they would encounter. They did not return, and a year later their brother Charles, who had gone in search of them, found their decapitated bodies lying near the river.

Some years later a prospector named Jorgensson, looking for gold, was also found dead. In 1926, Annie Laferte started out from Fort Simpson to explore the Nahanni River and was never seen again. Two years later yet annother victim was claimed, a prospector named Fisher, whose bleaching bones were found by a search party. A few months later another expedition started up the river, and all three members were later found dead. In 1936, two more died: in 1940, Ollie Golmberg, of Edmonton, vanished without trace. Since then others have disappeared.

For nearly half a century these mysterious happenings have continued, and the valley continues to uphold its reputation of awe and dread.

But we now know that there was a considerable amount of truth in the tales told by the Indians. In 1927 an aeroplane landed in the valley and its occupants found themselves in a hot, steamy atmosphere where vegetation grew luxuriantly. Clouds of steam arose from hot springs and pools, and the whole place was so warm and fertile that it was easy to perceive how the legend of the "tropical valley" had arisen. To hungry Indian hunters it must have appeared as a haven of refuge amid the snowy peaks of this sub-Arctic wilderness.

Another Indian legend told of "the great falling waters", whose roaring could be heard twenty miles away. To investigate this story, a year later, Mr. F. Hunter, F.R.G.S., and two companions, started up the South Nahanni River in a canoe. A hundred and twenty miles from the mouth of the river they came upon a waterfall which they named the Virginia Falls. It proved to be the highest waterfall in Canada on a river of any size, for here the Nahanni plunged over a sheer cliff nearly three hundred and twenty feet high. Hunter believed that they were the first white men ever to view the great cataract.

Another discovery was made in 1933 when Mr. Edward Clausen reported the discovery of caves containing the remains of human beings of Mongol type. Another explorer, W. L. Bliss, after studying the caverns, produced a theory that they had been used as dwelling-places by the ancestors of the American Indians during their migration from Asia thousands of years ago. We know that the ancestors of the present inhabitants of America came from Asia by way of

Bering Strait long before the arrival of Columbus, and the Nahanni Valley might well have been one of the places where a migrating people could settle for a time before moving on.

Although these discoveries provide us with the factual basis of the old Indian legends, they do not help us to solve the sequence of mysterious deaths which have taken place in the valley. Various theories have been advanced, one of the most interesting being that put forward by Mr. Donald Caroll, of the United States Geological Survey, when he visited the area three years ago. He maintained that the original population of the valley had been wiped out by an epidemic of virulent staphylococcus type of meningitis.

"The half-ruined stone huts are still standing," he reported, "and whoever takes shelter in them contracts the extremely infectious disease. The bacteria is of the type which can remain dormant for a considerable time. It appears that when trappers, hunters and prospectors were in the region they naturally sought the shelter of the huts which were still standing. The warmth of the camp-fires would quickly rouse the bacteria from its dormant state."

Travellers would soon become too ill to move on, he concluded, and without proper medical attention they would die. A doctor is said to have made a special journey to the valley to get samples of the bacteria, and either prove or disprove this theory, but whether he succeeded in his aim we have no means of knowing.

Trappers and prospectors who know the Nahanni country are sceptical of this theory, as many of the human remains discovered show all too clearly evidence of foul play. Beings capable of handling a knife and a gun killed the luckless explorers, they maintain.

And so we get back to our original speculations about the valley. Is it really populated by the remnants of a strange prehistoric race, who may be headhunters and cannibals? Or are they merely primitive Indian tribesmen who prefer to live the simple life rather than enjoy the doubtful benefits of civilization? Or is the valley a refuge for certain persons who are wanted for various crimes, and who kill anyone who discovers the locality of their hiding-place? That, at least, is the generally agreed theory in north-western Canada.

Canada has other records of hidden valleys and lost tribes, which, as yet, science has neither proved nor disproved. There are vast areas of country which are almost completely unexplored, among the so-called "Barren Lands" of the North-West Territories and the wooded mountain country of the Pacific Coast. For the archaeologist there is an almost virgin field awaiting investigation.

Ships have been sailing into Hudson Bay, for instance, for over three hundred years, and one would think that during this time the area would have been thoroughly explored. Yet it was not until some years after the First World War that a big island seventy miles long was discovered in the Bay. Though sighted by passing ships for centuries, it had never been properly explored, but simply recorded on the maps as a group of scattered islands.

In British Columbia are several areas where the explorer may well make some interesting and unusual discoveries. Within two hundred miles of Vancouver there are mountain ranges twelve thousand feet or more high, which have not been mapped, named, climbed, perhaps not even seen by white men. In the forested central portion of Vancouver Island is the Forbidden Plateau, said to be inhabited by a remote, secretive Indian race, who practise strange rites and have no contact with the outside world. Observers report that at certain times of the year signal fires can be seen blazing among the inaccessible peaks of this lost world plateau, as if to summon these unknown people to meeting or worship.

Similar signal fires have been reported among the high peaks of the Chehalis Range, on the mainland, and are believed to summon the mysterious Sasquatch tribesmen to their secret meeting-places. These Sasquatch are one of the enigmas of modern exploration in Canada. Though there is a considerable amount of information about them, no trained scientist has observed them and there is no circumstantial evidence to prove they exist.

The Sasquatch are said to be a race of giant cave-dwellers who live in the rugged mountain country about a hundred miles east of Vancouver. They were said to vary from six-and-a-half to seven feet in height, being broad-shouldered, long armed and hideous-looking. Descriptions of them have been reported from time to time, at infrequent intervals. I quote a description from a letter written by a Mr. Herbert Point who encountered one of these strange people near the little mountain town of Agassiz: "He was twice as big as the average man, with hands so long they nearly touched the ground, and his nose seemed spread all over his face. His body was covered with hair like an animal. He stopped within fifty feet of us. We ran away as fast as we could."

The fear inspired by the sudden appearance of these huge, hairy, naked men usually results in only a very general description of them being available. But reports of such meetings now go back several decades, the witnesses often being persons whose truthfulness there is no reason to doubt. An Indian half-breed named Peter Williams living on the Chehalis Indian reservation, stated that he encountered a creature which he took to be a bear, but which proved to be a man between six and seven feet tall, covered with hair.

"I turned and ran through the under-brush to my dug-out," he stated. "The hairy man came after me. I paddled across the stream, which is not very deep, and the man waded after me. I reached the house where my wife and child were inside. I bolted the door. Presently the hairy man arrived. It was growing dark. He prowled about, grunting and growling, but after a little while he went away." A day or so later the half-breed's brother was out fishing when he was accosted by a big hairy man who drove him away and stole his fish.

An Indian named Thomas Cedar was out fishing on a tributary of the Harrison River when a huge rock fell into the water so close to his canoe that it was nearly overturned. He looked up and saw a huge hairy man standing on the bank, about to hurl another rock. The Indian managed to paddle out of the way quickly enough to avoid having his canoe sunk. He fled back to the settlement, and did not go fishing in that place again.

According to an Indian legend, this river was the scene of a battle between two bands of Sasquatch, who fought until the race was almost exterminated. A Captain Warde, who had resided in the district for a number of years, was informed that the stream had been known as the Saskakau River when the first white settlers arrived. Some caves near the river bank were said to be the home of the hairy giants. Captain Warde explored the caves and reported that they showed evidence of having been lived in, and that there were crude drawings on the walls.

There are other reports of similar encounters too numerous to mention here.

The Chehalis Indians have oral records going back three generations, and state that in the spring of every fourth year a fire is seen burning on one of the highest peaks of the mountains. It burns for four nights in succession, then is not seen for another four years. Sometimes there is only one single column of smoke rising, sometimes several, which rise and fall as though a message is being sent out. The Indians believe that this is a signal to the scattered groups of Sasquatch to meet at a certain place in the mountains, perhaps for the purpose of worshipping at some ancient shrine.

Although scientists attached to the museum at Vancouver are sceptical concerning the existence of this race of giant, hairy men, they cannot state definitely that they do not exist. Too often have recent discoveries proved that truth is, indeed, stranger than fiction, and demonstrated that what is believed to be impossible has, in fact, actually happened.

The descriptions in this book of such places as the "Lost Valley" discovered during the last war in Dutch New Guinea, or the Khevsoors, descendants of twelfth-century Crusaders, are evidence that this is true. Those persons who relegate accounts of the Sasquatch to the realms of the sea-serpent or the lost continent of Atlantis and such uninvestigated phenomena, should consider the credibility of the witnesses. What have they to gain by inventing such stories? Usually the eye-witness reports have only been secured with reluctance, for the Indians are as sensitive to ridicule as white men, and would prefer to keep accounts of the Sasquatch to themselves rather than risk having their word doubted.

In conclusion, then, the evidence amounts to this: that in the unexplored mountain wilderness of British Columbia there may be the remnants of an unknown race of hairy giants. That at intervals of a few years they meet at some ancient shrine of their race. That their migration to these ancient meeting-places takes them across country which is now becoming settled and civilized, and therefore encounters with present-day inhabitants are more frequent. Beyond these statements we cannot go.

But at any time now some patient investigator may stumble upon a discovery which will shed new light on this hypothesis. Canada offers plenty of scope for archaeologists and anthropologists seeking new worlds to conquer.

PART TWO

CENTRAL AMERICA and SOUTH AMERICA

Central America

I

THE CITY OF THE SACRED WELL

"*What* books or persons would you choose to have with you, if you were fated to be shipwrecked on a desert island?" is a very popular Quiz question. As I cannot imagine any possible happiness resulting from a perpetual sight of Miss Betty Grable's legs, nor of listening for months, perhaps years, to Dr. Samuel Johnson, I have myself not the slightest interest in such a question. And I cannot say either that I long to live for months with a volume of Shakespeare's plays as company.

When my imagination does toy with these impossible speculations, it turns to the periods and places in which I would have liked to have led one of my former reincarnated lives. I am quite sure one of these would be amidst the grandeur of the Mayan civilization when it was at its height.

Next to the Greeks, I would place the Mayans (and possibly the Khmers) in second place as the most civilized (in the best sense of this word) race which has ever populated this world. But this is not a matter to discuss here, and I only mention it because it brings me to the wonderful dead city of Chi-chen Itza in Yucatan.

This was a city that covered an area of over a dozen square miles and had, at its zenith, a population approaching a million persons. It was a city of great palaces, temples, mausoleums; a city of untold treasures and wealth. Yet its greatness vanished almost in a night. No one knows whether its thousands of inhabitants perished by the sword or abandoned their homes for some reason. Nobody knows; for all this took place before Columbus arrived in America.

If you look at a map you will see that Yucatan is that

southern part of Mexico, ending like the upflung tail of a large fish, which juts into the great Gulf of Mexico. On the map you will also see that Progreso is the main port (a place one should plan to leave at the earliest possible moment), distant some twenty-four miles from the very delightful capital of the province, Mérida. From this latter city, Chichen Itza, which lies in the eastern part of Yucatan, can be reached by train and automobile.

The journey is well worth while, for here, lying in dense jungle, is one of the most remarkable dead cities of the world. Here was the Holy City, the Mecca of all the ancient Mayan people, and here you can still see many wonderful buildings, some of them in perfect preservation, although they have not been in use for nearly one thousand years.

Actually there are the ruins of two cities, the older of which has almost completely disappeared, for its stones were ruthlessly used to create the second and newer city in about A.D. 1200. It is then, this newer city which provides the interest, for here are to be found many remarkable buildings, some of which retain their original roofs and are still habitable.

There is the three-storied *La Casa del Monjas* or the Nunnery. This may have been a building for housing nuns, or it may have been a training-school for priests. It is a rambling building, with many annexes, and is exquisite in its architectural harmony and very richly ornamented. It certainly ranks as one of the most wonderfully carved edifices in Yucatan.

Rising in three reducing tiers to a total height of nearly 90 feet, the frontage of the main building at ground level is 228 feet. Inside the vast building are many rooms, the main ones being long and narrow, and having alcoves which appear to have been the Mayan equivalent for book-cases, or may have contained idols.

The approach to the second tier is by a grand stone stairway of 40 steps, and 40 feet wide. Another wide staircase leads to the top tier, where the building is now in a ruined state.

In the interior of this great building there is much ornamentation and symbolic carving, the dominant motif being the representation of the god, Kukul Can. The mask of this strange god is shown with an upturned snout, rather like an elephant's trunk. The general impression throughout this unique building is of grace and beauty.

Another unique building, situated on the highest point in the city, is known as the *caracol* or "Snail-shell". It consists of a round tower, 40 feet high, within which there is a small chamber, placed on a large, built-up terrace, 20 feet in height. It is thought that this building may have been used for astronomical observations or it may have been merely a watch-tower. Its commanding position would have enabled the watchers, for instance, to spot immediately any outbreak of fire in the surrounding city.

Best preserved of all the buildings at Chi-chen Itza is the *Chich-an Chob* or Red House. It gets its name from the broad red band painted round the four walls of its vestibule. Except for the absence of pillars, this building would pass for a gem of Doric architecture.

The religious centre of the city was probably in the *El Castillo*, shaped like a pyramid and rising to a height of about 80 feet. Here the worship of the god, Kukul Can, was carried out and the dominant feature is serpents, for they are to be found carved in stone on all sides. The principal staircase is guarded by two huge heads of feathered serpents, jaws open, fangs displayed, and forked tongues extended. These remarkable statues are carved from single blocks of stone and are perfectly executed. In front of the main entrance to this temple there once stood a great stone slab or altar (now lost) supported by curious stone figures and strange male caryatids, which still stand. The interesting feature of the figures is that they represent bearded men.

Who, then, were their prototypes? For the Mayans are beardless. Were they some shipwrecked Norsemen of the old Viking days, or Atlanteans, whose country Plato says "sank in one day and one night beneath the waves of the ocean"?

It was at this temple that the most important religious rites were doubtless performed, including solemn invocations to the sun.

Nearby is the Temple of the Tiger, taking its name from the frieze of bas-reliefs showing the jaguar as the motif. These sculptures are one of the outstanding treasures of the lost art of the Mayans. Its wonderful carvings have caught the grace of the animals represented. Inside this temple the walls are covered with paintings of battle scenes, sacrificial pageants, and domestic life. The colours are as brilliant now as the day they were painted. All these pictures are cleverly drawn, in excellent proportion, elaborately coloured, and each is different.

Undoubtedly this temple is the prize exhibit of Chi-chen Itza, not because of its size, but for its perfect craftsmanship and the charm displayed in every detail of its decoration. With two other buildings, the Temple of the Tiger forms part of a large courtyard, 420 feet in length, which is bounded by enormous, perpendicular stone walls 20 feet in height and 30 feet wide at the base. This great courtyard was doubtless connected with religious ceremonies. Facing the northern extremity of this block of buildings is a small temple containing a single chamber. Against the centre of its rear wall is the perfect figure of a bearded man having strong Hebraic features. Again one wonders how the origin of this design arose.

One other building deserves mention. It is the great tennis court or gymnasium. It is known that the Aztecs, who overcame the Mayans as occupiers of Chi-chen Itza, played a form of this game, using a hard, wooden ball. Prior to the start of a series of these games there were held religious ceremonies.

I now come to one of the most interesting features of this Mayan city—the great wells. Water supply must always form one of the major problems to be solved in the management of any city or town. In the case of Chi-chen Itza the problem was overcome by the use of three great wells. The largest of these, known as the Sacred Well, is a great natural pit, of elliptical shape, 250 feet long and about 160 feet wide. The drop from the ground surface to the water level is 70 feet. The supply of water is almost limitless.

For many years an American archaeologist, Mr. Edward

Herbert Thompson, has carried out investigations at Chichen Itza, and he spent a considerable time in dredging the Sacred Well. This took its name from the fact that maidens and sometimes captive warriors were hurled into its waters with the object of propitiating Yum Chac, the Rain God.

From its depths many interesting objects have been recovered. There were numerous articles made of rubber; for the use of this natural product was known in this part of the world long before it became an essential material in our civilization. There were an early people living in what is now Mexico who were known as the *Hulmecas*, or "rubber people", because of their great skill in adapting it to everyday use.

Hundreds of skulls, also, have been recovered, many of them being those of young females. There have been, too, treasures of every kind: ornamental bells, gold filigrees of exquisite design, copper and gold disks showing the Sun God, tiaras, brooches, pottery, wooden toys, and jade ornaments. It is interesting to surmise how jade came to be found in this part of the world, for it is not indigenous to America.

Jade actually was the most precious treasure known to the Mayan, Aztec and Incan civilizations. These great races regarded silver as being of no value, gold as being useful merely for decorative purposes, and it was jade that was held in high esteem.

It is recorded that when Montezuma, the ruler of the Incas, was under what we would now term "house arrest", he used to play nightly with Cortés a native game which resembled chess. At the conclusion of each night's play both sides courteously exchanged presents. When these gifts were gold objects, Cortés was naturally pleased. One night, however, Montezuma informed the Spaniard that he was to receive a very special gift. This turned out to be a jade ornament, which Cortés courteously accepted, although it meant little to him. The jade relics thrown into the Sacred Well were doubtless regarded by their donors as being the most precious of offerings.

Particularly interesting were the sacrificial knives or dart throwers which were brought up from the depths. And there were the "throwing-sticks" (*hul-che*), minutely carved and, inlaid with superb workmanship. The Mayans did not use bows and arrows, but made use of these "throwing-sticks" with great effect. A powerful overhead motion of the arm released a dart— a weapon of death. Constant practice made its use highly effective.

It was not an easy task for Mr. Thompson to recover many of these objects. Ordinary dredging methods failed to explore effectively the uneven floor of the Sacred Well. It was only when diving was resorted to that the great finds were made. As a result of this American's work, spread over many years and at considerable cost, we know much more about this greatest of Mayan cities. Many American museums are the richer for the exquisite treasures recovered from the depths of those jade-blue waters.

LAST OF THE AZTECS

The three great races which once occupied much that is now Mexico and Central America were the Toltecs, the Mayas, and the Aztecs. The Toltecs were a people who according to tradition preceded the Aztecs; and they were specially associated with the ruins at Teotihuacan, a site about twenty-five miles from Mexico City. According to legend they were the introducers of the arts and culture to Mexico, from whom the Aztecs learned them.

The Mayas (the "Greeks" of this ancient world) were another highly cultured race. I have given in the last chapter one example of their skill, but there are many others, for in Yucatan are still to be found the remains of other great monuments, palaces, temples and pyramids. At the present time the race is represented strongly in Yucatan, where the language is still spoken.

The Aztecs were the "Romans" of Central America. They were primarily warriors and organizers. They found little difficulty in forcibly overcoming the peace-loving Mayas and other tribes, thus building up a powerful empire which endured for some centuries before it was overthrown by the Spaniards under Cortés in 1520.

Following their defeat, the remnants of the Aztecs scattered and were gradually absorbed into the local native populations so that there is no distinct Aztec race left today. However, an interesting remnant is still to be found in the Guaymis, a tribe living in the wildest and unexplored part of northern Panama.

Most people get their ideas of this country from what they see as they pass through the great canal which traverses it. It appears thoroughly "civilized", for the Canal Zone comes under the control of the United States. But in the hinterland there are the "forbidden" districts where the Panamanian Government has little and often no control. Here are primitive and savage tribes, independent and hostile, who have never yet been conquered. Even the Spaniards who tried to subdue them in the past and carried on a relentless war, finally gave up the struggle as hopeless.

Few white men have gone into the interior and come back alive, but those that have returned safely reported that the Guaymis were not unfriendly, although at first highly suspicious of any intruder. These people, in fact, retain the mentality of their ancestors, the Aztecs, of whom they are direct descendants.

Their chiefs still wear the ancient head-dresses of feathers obtained from the resplendent *trogan* or Quetzal, the sacred bird of the Aztecs. In physical appearance, too, they resemble the one-time rulers of Central America, being of small stature, broad-featured, of reddish-brown skin, and lean. They alone still use the ancient Aztec spear, the "throwing-stick". With the Aztecs this weapon was called the "atlatl" while with the Guaymis it is known as the "m'adtli".

The Guaymis are very fond of adorning themselves in a manner which would certainly cause most investigating explorers to retrace their steps back to civilization. They wear garments made of highly decorative cloths, while round their necks hang necklaces composed of jaguar and pecary teeth, human scalp locks, and other strange fetishes. Their faces are painted with elaborate patterns, marked out in vivid reds and black.

Hyatt Verrill, a well-known traveller and writer of the past, once made a journey into the land of the Guaymis. It is true that he did not get very far into the country, but he was received quite kindly. In fact, because he cured "miraculously" an important personage of the colic, he was elected to be a fully-fledged member of the tribe with the rank of medicine-man.

In his honour and to celebrate the event, a special ceremony was held. When he was forcibly siezed and dragged to what appeared to be a sacrificial altar, he quite naturally thought his last hour had come. But this was simply part of the service of initiation into tribal membership.

The ceremony was then followed by a display of the "stick dance". This dance is held only at night, with torches aflame and under a full moon. The sticks used are seven-foot poles, three inches in diameter, and pointed at one end. The dance itself is really a form of contest between two performers. One man takes a spear which he hurls at the other contestant, trying to secure a body hit. If the man who is attacked manages to avoid the spear, he then changes places and becomes the stick-thrower. The only protection provided for the contestants is the stuffed skin of an animal which is strapped on the back to protect the spine.

When the Spaniards first arrived in America this game was generally popular, but because of its dangers it was forbidden. It is now found as an active amusement only with this tribe.

The Guaymis too still use the Aztec method of "writing" messages. This consists in taking plaited cords of palm leaf and tying it into a variety of knots. The arrangement and type of these knots conveys the message desired. When an important chief, therefore, wishes to convey orders or instructions throughout the land, he simply causes a required number of knotted strings to be made, which are then handed over to selected messengers, with faces specially painted to indicate their job, and with these they race off to their destinations.

The ancient Spaniards were often surprised at the rapidity with which news was conveyed to distant places, but this quite simple method is the answer.

Despite his membership of the tribe, Mr. Hyatt Verrill was never allowed to penetrate far into the country of the Guaymis. It was always arranged that people should come to him at his camp on the border and never that he should visit them. On one occasion his attempt to take a photograph of a tribesman nearly brought about his death. Here then seems to be an interesting field of exploration for some courageous traveller.

South America

I

HEAD-HUNTERS OF THE AMAZON

In the days of one's youth what adventures one can have . . .

It was the shrunken head, little bigger than an orange, the trophy of a man-hunt in the interior of Ecuador, which first sowed the seeds of interest in my mind. This head was an exhibit in a museum in Paris, which shows how prosaically, but realistically, one's life can be directed. For I carried in my mind a longing to see the people who indulged in this rather horrible art.

A couple of years later I chanced to be in Bolivia working on a tin mine. At the conclusion of my contract I travelled north, and because of some engine trouble on the ship in which I was a passenger found myself delayed in Chiclayo *en route* to Guayaquil.

Chiclayo, which is in Peru, is definitely the most ghastly spot in which I have ever been stranded—and I can name some pretty horrible places I have encountered. It was, therefore, as an alternative to the appalling humid heat and the boredom I was experiencing which led me into a fantastic journey into the interior; especially as this journey aimed at visiting the land of the Jivaros, or Jeveros, in Peru.

The Jivaros remain even to-day a thoroughly savage and uncivilized race. They seldom come into contact with the white man and, owing to their inaccessibility, the government has no practical control over them. They live in a country which is most inhospitable in its climate and consists of dense, trackless jungle.

I will not relate here the adventures of the journey I made

into the interior along with my companion. Suffice it to say
that it embraced a series of most thrilling adventures. In
due course we did reach a Jivaro village, only to find it
unoccupied, although we had the uncanny feeling that we
were being watched by unseen persons. It was our fire-arms
which gave us protection.

In this deserted village the most important building was
the communal dwelling-house, a large hut measuring about
fifty feet by sixteen. It was divided on the ground floor into
various compartments, rather like horse-boxes. Each of these
was the home of one family. Over these "boxes" ran a platform where the people used to sit and work. The whole of
the centre of the hut was reserved for communal activities
and for cooking.

One of the first things we found were small cages in
which there were heads that were undergoing a reduction
in size. I saw some four heads. There were also lying about
some Jivaro weapons: blow-guns and javelins, for bows and
arrows are seldom used, and only a few of the Jivaros have
been able to procure muskets from traders. The javelins
were strongly made of wood about eight feet in length, and
the ends are tipped with iron. The blow-guns were of the
same length, being made of palm-wood. The darts used
were just over six inches long and about one-tenth of an
inch in diameter. The darts are carried in small cylindrical
cases made of bamboo. A mere whiff of breath forces them
at their objective, and the Jivaros have acquired extreme
skill at scoring bull's-eyes.

The Jivaros wage a constant warfare among themselves,
for which polygamy is the direct cause. We were later told
that when a girl arrives at the marriageable age, about
twelve to fourteen years, she is given in marriage by her
father to some friend, but most of the wives are gained by
the killing of an enemy and the confiscation of the women as
the spoils of war. Thus a man may have from five to eight
wives.

The warfare may be against a member of a neighbouring
tribe or against a fellow-Jivaro living at some distance. The
women and children of the slain man are adopted into the

household of the victor, where they become members of the family, and are treated in the same manner as the immediate family, and not as slaves.

These Indians have a pseudo-religion which is based on a belief in a being called by the Spaniards *el diablo*, the devil. He has the attributes of a super-Jivaro, is all-powerful in everything he undertakes, but is not particularly addicted to evil for its own sake.

No important project is undertaken without first consulting *el diablo* and getting his views. The Jivaros do not seem to have developed a priest class, so any man may enter into consultation with him. To do this, it is necessary to retire to the seclusion of some spot remote from the rest of the Jivaros, and here the would-be communicant prepares himself for the ordeal by drinking a quantity of an extract made from a particular variety of bark. This fluid is dark, about the colour of coffee, and contains some very powerful narcotic, for it produces a stupor and hallucinations, of a different type but in a way comparable to the result produced by the use of opium or hemp.

While under the influence of this drink, which may last for four or five hours, the Jivaro imagines that the devil comes to him and discusses whatever matter is afoot. Inasmuch as the mind of the man is filled with his plans when he takes the narotic, it is but natural that his disordered reason concocts a fanciful dialogue and arrives at a confirmation of what he really believed when he first came.

If the devil has properly coached his client and the raid is eminently successful, the hut of the victim is surrounded, and when the latter steps out of his door he receives at close range the contents of the blow-guns of the party. The women and children are hastily captured and the raiders seek safety in their own neighbourhood, with the reasonable assurance that sooner or later they will be raided in a like manner by relatives of the slain man.

The head of the victim is cut off, and later, in the seclusion of his hut, the victor prepares it into a lasting war trophy, attaching to it a significance which the North American Indian attached to scalps. The skin is opened up from the

62

base of the neck to the crown, and the skull is removed entire, leaving only the soft, pliant skin.

The skin is now dipped into a vegetable extract which dyes it a blue-black and probably has some action as a preservative, and then the cut skin is sewn up along the neck to restore the head to its original shape.

The cavity is filled with hot sand òr pebbles, after which the head is constantly turned and moved, so that the drying goes on uniformly. When the sand has cooled, more hot sand takes its place, and this process may last for several days before the head is completely cured.

Shrinking to an unbelievable degree takes place, but it is so regulated that the features retain their individuality to a great extent, and the finished head is about the size of a man's fist.

The lips have been sewed shut with a series of long cotton cords, the exact pattern of this stitching varying with the locality and seeming to have some significance. Within a short time after the preparation of a head, generally within a month, the victor celebrates the event by a ceremonial dance at which there is an orgy of wild drinking. After this dance it may be possible to buy the head from the Jivaro, if his interest can be aroused in an object whose value he understands and appreciates, such as a musket.

Because of the interest aroused in the outside world by tales concerning these head-hunters, there has been in the past a certain trade in human heads. The Jivaros, learning that there was this demand which could be capitalized into muskets, quickly gave a ready response; so that it became necessary for the Ecuadorean Government strictly to forbid the traffic in these gruesome objects.

I did hear one story which was not without a certain grim irony. It concerned a red-headed white man who went into the interior on a trip of exploration with the commision of bringing out a dried and shrunken head. It was months after he had departed that a shrunken head came out, by devious channels, from the interior, but the head had red hair. Perhaps a red-haired head brought the price of two muskets; who can tell?

Contrary to expectation, after hearing stories of the Jivaros (and down at the coast the word Jivaro is synonymous with violent death), we found them, when we got to know them, a good-natured people and very friendly to us.

But before we did make friends with them, they tried to harm us. As I have already related, we found their village deserted on our arrival; but before long a shower of little darts fell on us. Fortunately our clothes protected our skins against any evil effects. My companion and I then fired in the direction of the dart-blowers. That was enough to prove our superiority. A few minutes later several of the dreaded Jivaros crept out of the surrounding jungle.

They were short men, but with a splendid chest development and with rather a pleasing countenance. They wear their hair long, but often cut it away to form a fringe in front, and it is ornamented with tufts of bright red and yellow toucan feathers on the crown and at the base of the neck. The men wear slender tubes of bamboo thrust through the lobes of the ears and the women often have a short piece of cane projecting straight out from the lower lip. The men we met wore as their only clothing a piece of cloth about two feet long suspended from a waist-band.

Although they had tried to kill us, they now showed no signs of fear and walked about freely, talking to each other. It was a peculiar kind of talk, being in a sing-song voice which died away almost to a silence at the end of each sentence. Throughout each sentence—almost at every other word—the speaker spat on the ground. The Jivaro language is a highly complicated one for strangers to understand. In the words of the late and ever-missed Marie Lloyd's famous song, "Every little movement has a meaning of its own", and so it is with the Jivaro tongue. Not only do they have their spoken language, but they also include in their "talk" a great variety of signs and movements of the body. It is a combination of words and movements which expresses their meanings. They are very clever at imitating birds and animals, so much so that they can even lure them within range when they are immediately shot at either by lance or blow-pipe.

As hunters and woodsmen the Jivaros are unsurpassed. Their chief occupation is roaming the jungle in search of game. The poison used for their "ammunition" is a form of curare, an extract of *Strychnos toxifera* and other South American plants. It is very potent, death resulting in a few minutes after an animal has been struck; but the use of it does not spoil the game for human consumption. Salt is said to be an antidote, if placed in the mouth of the stricken animal, and monkeys are sometimes taken alive in this manner, the Jivaro hurrying up to administer the panacea when the quarry falls from the limb of a tree in a stupor.

Another poison extensively used by the Jivaros is *barbasco*, a jungle vine or creeper, which is put into the rivers to secure fish. A great pile of the plant is beaten up on the rocks until it is a pulp, and after the Indians have stationed themselves down-stream some of their number throw a couple of hundred pounds or so of the mash into the river. Then the fishing begins. The fish are killed and float down, belly up, to be gathered in by the Jivaros who see them as they pass. So potent is this juice that large streams may be poisoned by a relatively small amount of *barbasco*, and under favourable circumstances fish are stricken for a distance of three miles down-stream.

The men we saw appeared to treat their women kindly and showed a consideration for their wishes in minor matters. If the wife is detected in any breach of infidelity, however, she is subjected to a most severe course of discipline. For the first offence the punishment consists in throwing the erring woman to the ground, holding her there and cutting down on to the crown of her head with a large machete or brush knife. The man administering the punishment, usually the husband, makes a great many cuts, which are at an angle to one another, so that the scalp is literally hacked into small pieces and all the hair lost.

Should this not prove sufficient to inculcate fidelity, the second offence results in the woman being pinned to the earth by a long, iron-pointed lance, which is thrust deep into the ground through the fleshy parts of both legs. Given food, water, and sufficient care to prevent death, the offender is left in this position for days, even for a period as long as three weeks.

For the third offence the punishment is death outright, but as one Jivaro laughingly told us, it is very seldom that this penalty is inflicted.

We were able to converse quite well with the Jivaros, for we had with us a Spanish half-caste guide. It happened that two of the Jivaros in the camp where we were also spoke Spanish. However, we found the way in which these natives kept handling our guns a considerable nuisance. To them they obviously represented the highest form of wealth, and there is little doubt that if we had not maintained the strictest security precautions we might have been killed simply for our guns.

We spent three days in the Jivaro settlement. Our original intention had been to make our way through to Iquitos on the Amazon in Brazil. But it was obvious that the project was quite impossible; so early one morning we set out on the trail by which we had come. It was with a sense of considerable relief that we arrived once more in Jaen, the first outpost of civilization, and found ourselves again sleeping between sheets.

TIAHUANACO—OLDEST CITY OF THE NEW WORLD

Bolivia has some of the oldest ruins and the highest navigable lake in the Western Hemisphere. Lake Titicaca lies two and a half miles above the sea, and on its southern edge and the border of Bolivia, where the village of Tiahuanaco is now situated, there are in the vicinity the ruins of the city of Tiahuanaco, the oldest city of the New World.

No one knows the true history of Tiahuanaco, for its carvings and its characters have never been read with certainty. The city's ruins are now some miles from the waters of the lake, but in the long-distant past it is evident that it lay actually beside it, the waters having gradually receded through the course of centuries.

Tiahuanaco has been judged the product of two distinct and successive civilizations, the latter supposedly reconstructing, to some extent, ruins left by an earlier people. Some investigators attribute the reconstruction work to the Aymaras, whose descendants now live in the region, but the latter have no traditions or legends about such builders, much less of the primitive preceding civilization.

The theory has been advanced that the origin of the Tiahuanacotans derives from an ancient Andean race of Mongoloid ancestry, contemporary with the predecessors of the founders of the Mayan civilization in Central America. Certainly the present-day Aymara Indians have a startling resemblance to the Asiatic Mongols. The Aymara tongue is the Sanskrit of America, and even older than Tiahuanaco; but the Aymara race itself, conquered by the language and taking its name from it, is far younger.

There are many indications that two different civilizations succeeded each other at ancient Tiahuanaco. Many of the worked stones are only half finished, which induces the belief that some great catastrophe, natural or otherwise, compelled the workmen to leave their task incomplete.

The character of the work itself denotes that the half-shaped and sculptured stones belong to the second phase of Tiahuanaco's history. Statues and monoliths are not of the same rock materials, nor of the same artistic style. Some are of the grey-grained arsenic stone, almost as enduring as flint, while others are of red sandstone, more enduring than one might think. The latter would seem to be of the second epoch; and this is the stone in which one finds the unfinished work.

Great monoliths enclose an enormous quadrangle to the east of the present village, and these have a very striking resemblance to Stonehenge.

Dolmens, or stone tables, generally consisting of three or four large flat stones, covered with another and larger one, like a table supported by its legs, are found in many places about this region, but more especially near the shores of Lake Titicaca and upon its many islands.

These may be the remains of what once were tombs of heroes and notable persons to whom the tribe wished to pay tribute. They are similar in appearance to those seen in Denmark, France and other European countries. Covered galleries, with their openings always toward the rising sun or to the north, are occasionally found in neighbouring low hills.

Other features of these monuments are the great statues hewn out of the raw stone, representing heroes and divinities, a class of sculpture entirely lacking among European ruins of comparable culture.

One of the most important ruins, called Akapana, rises to a height of 165 feet. The base is an irregular parallelogram, with the four sides duly placed towards the four cardinal points. Its flattened surface, with sloping sides, makes it a sort of truncated pyramid. Apparently it once stood in the midst of a series of pyramids, but these have been considerably destroyed.

The side walls, about 485 feet by 650 feet, were made of huge joined rectangular rocks, with smaller ones solidifying the whole, but great quantities of the latter have been removed by the Indians and used for their own building purposes, until the whole work has become a ruin of ruins. A stairway once led to the upper level where a great basin of water stood. A canal of stone seems to have led down the side of this mound, for some purpose not now clear. Whether this mountain-type of building was the centre of religious worship, a place for sacrifice, the home of monarchs, or a place of defence, will probably never be known.

Four hundred yards north of Akapana lies the oldest of the ruins, Kalasasaya, or Temple of the Sun. It is a parallelogram about 400 feet square, marked on all sides by upright menhirs from 15 to 20 feet high. This ruin rises from a single terrace about 10 feet above the surrounding plain, which is said to have been covered entirely with smooth paving stones at one time, but these have been removed almost completely by the local inhabitants.

Monolith and statue bases, tops of great pillars, conduit sections, and other pieces still remain, but this whole ruin is one great, silent testimony to the unthinking expediency of Aymara Indians, nearly everything movable having been taken. In times past troops have even been quartered among the ruins and have practised their markmanship on the priceless relics.

Pillars are deeply rooted in the soil and so cut and designed as to bear great slabs, platforms, and arches. They are from 16 to 20 feet apart. Even where their tops are not chiselled and sculptured they are nearly the same height, making it apparent that they once bore the lintels and other pieces of structural stone.

The entrace to this ruin is on the east by a stone stairway of eight broad, well-preserved steps, flanked at the foot by two monoliths and leading up to the level of the quadrangle. In the north-western angle of Kalasasaya the Great Portal, Sanctuary, or Gateway of the Sun, as it is variously known, is the most interesting single portion of the ruins to the east of the village. Once recumbent, it is now standing upright, restored, though unfortunately broken through the upper section by a bolt of lightning (it is thought), and the two parts rest obliquely against each other.

This famous door, like others of Tiahuanaco, was shaped from a single block of grey volcanic rock about 16 inches thick. Standing erect, it measures some 11 by 15 feet and faces toward the east. The surprising façade is wonderfully ornamented in low relief upon the eastern side above the door. The western face is comparatively plain. The motif of the ornamentation consists in general of a figure of the Sun God, the rays about his head, some of which terminate in small heads of a jaguar, the Tiahuanaco God of Night, and bearer of the moon in the sky.

In each hand the Sun God bears a hoe-shaped sceptre. He is flanked by fourty-eight figures, twenty-four on each side, consisting of eight figures each, these being about a quarter his own size. The figures all face the god, are running towards him, in fact, and carry small sceptres similar to his. Upper and lower rows on either hand bear the likeness of a winged man, and all are crowned alike, being repetitions of a single figure. The middle row of figures on either side, consisting of sixteen, also a repetition of one figure, are like the others save for the head, which ends in a strong curved beak, representing the condor, royal bird of the Andes, now appearing on Bolivia's coat of arms.

According to a Tiahuanacotan legend, a giant condor bore the sun daily across the sky. The earliest pottery of the region shows this, and sometimes also a great condor in conflict with a jaguar or puma, typifying the conflict between Day and Night.

The figure of the Sun God rests upon a carved throne, below which another row of a different series of sixteen carved characters extends across the stone from side to side just over the doorway. These consist of small heads similar to the god's except that the features are in flat relief. Each is flanked by four condors' heads in plain relief, two pointing towards and two away from the face.

Many archaeologists have visited Tiahuanaco, but none has succeeded in deciphering the full meaning of the allegories and symbols of this celebrated monument. One investigator has hazarded the surmise that the sun is here suggested bearing the double sceptre of heat and light, with which he vivifies and dominates the world; that the crowned figures are of kings running towards him or the planets, his subalterns. They bear their own sceptres of power, but are subject to him, and their power is limited to that which each can wield in the solar system, while the great Sun God dominates them all. According to this theory the condors are messengers or ministers—comets, stars, and various planets more rapid than the others in their flight through space. Undoubtedly there is no better piece of stone-carving in the New World than this striking Gateway of the Sun.

East and west of Kalasasaya are several other ruins, neither so extensive nor so well preserved. Some individual specimens are especially interesting. One is a sacrificial stone, nearly square, hollowed in the centre, and with a groove which suggests that it may have been designed to accommodate the head and neck of sacrificial victims, probably sheep or young llamas, judging by the height of the aperture from the monument's base.

The ground has been cultivated up to the very margins of the ruins, while here and there great slabs recline or stand sturdily erect in the yellow barley stubble. Heavy doorways and their lintels have stood well where left alone, but most of them have been taken away to form entrances to Indian huts.

What a tale those magnificent slabs could tell if only they might have tongues! Yet as I wandered around the simple, present-day village with its mud huts, which blend into the landscape, I felt its surroundings intensified my realization of Tiahuanaco's great age. Neither the people now living there, nor their mode of living, can have greatly changed through the centuries. Shepherds still tend their flocks. Donkeys, cattle and sheep still graze peacefully in lowland meadows. An Aymara Indian drover with a train of llamas laden with llama-dung fuel starts off toward Illimani, bound for La Paz and its markets.

The other section of Tiahuanaco's ruins, known as Tuncapuncu (literally, The Ten Doors), is nearly a mile southwest of the others. The ruins lie upon a hill made by artificial means. It is about 50 feet above the surrounding plain, and the mound, about 150 feet square, slopes inward on all sides toward the east. The sides and most of the top of the hill are now under cultivation and probably have been for hundreds of years; yet the contours are still so uniform and clear that it seems obvious it must have served as a seating-place for a great audience intent on what was taking place in the structure near at hand.

Some experts claim that these ruins, known as the Palace of the Inca, once constituted a tribunal of justice. The four huge platforms, each made of a single stone, are supposed to have had ten lintels for ten doors, destined to support magnificent portals. It is all an architectural labyrinth, but the sculptured faces and the deities, which could be moved with tolerable ease, have been taken away; so that heroes and divinities, with other attractive smaller pieces, are no longer there. One can find some of them in museums and in the surrounding Indian homes.

The main parts of the rear of the temple must have been in great sections. Four well-defined ones are standing, and another, left unfinished, judging by the tracings, seems to have been added in Tiahuanaco's second epoch. The sections were probably bolted together with copper bars, since the bolt and bar channels in the stone are still plain, but the two main sections of each unit have parted or sunk. I mention copper here because this metal was worked by the Tiahuanacotans. Small copper implements are found in the ruins and the hills around contain much copper ore.

Volcanic stones are here carved and cut and grooved into sharp relief in a way both mysterious and beautiful. While most are decorated with a design of a severe yet graceful pattern, others plainly had some utilitarian purpose. There are pieces, for instance, that appear to have been basins, having apertures at the bottom through which water must have been discharged. There are plain and ornamented recesses which probably served as niches for idols to the sun, condor, jaguar, and other deities; and perhaps most interesting of all are the crosses sculptured on the backs of great blocks of stone. One can speculate endlessly. Certainly the carving of these blocks, which occurred from one to two thousand years ago, has nothing to do with the symbol introduced into Latin America with Christianity. These crosses are about 20 by 14 inches and may have been a detail in architecture, serving in place of masonry, since the reverse sides of the same blocks bear notches corresponding in dimensions to the lower part of the crosses.

Perhaps one of the most interesting coincidences is the occurrence of another form of cross, the swastika. While this type is not often seen in the architecture, it occurs in almost every form of the potters' art which has been excavated from the first epoch of Tiahuanaco's ruins. If the capital has the age some experts claim for it, here are some of the first examples of the use of the well-known good-luck or religious symbol.

Among the ruins of Tiahuanaco grey volcanic rock predominates. Probably the material for the capital was brought on great rafts across the lake from the sides of a nearby volcano. No one seems to know how these gigantic rocks were chiselled so well through their flint-like texture. They seem as if they might have been planed and bevelled, so fine of line are they.

A brief account of the two civilizations which once inhabited Tiahuanaco may be of interest. The earlier occupiers were, almost certainly, a great nation, and this was their capital from which they exercised control over a dominion of very great area. In time this race and their capital were attacked by the war-like invaders of the second period, who destroyed everything after conquering the city.

This conquering race was the Aymaras, ancestors of the present tribe living in this part of South America. However, the Aymara language is not directly connected with the race of that name; but it dates back to a very ancient period and was the tongue used by the original inhabitants. The invaders, in fact, when they conquered the land, were in turn conquered by the language, which they adopted and from which they took their own name.

To-day the pure Aymaras do not number half a million, yet they dominate the Bolivian Indian. The Aymara is war-like by nature and wedded to the soil only because of physical necessities, taking but poorly to governmental restrictions of any kind. The Aymaras of Tiahuanaco have little sentiment. Mud fences full of bits of human bone and fragments of pottery have been erected in fields where men fell during invasions.

Tiahuanaco is indeed a place in which one can dream. Here, in this lofty and now rather desolate plain, I tried to visualize what it must once have looked like when it was a great city in which flourished the most advanced of ancient American civilizations. As I sat on the Inca throne carved out of the natural rock I called up in my imagination a picture of the long-dead rulers watching their patient subjects labour at the construction of the magnificent walls of the fortress of Sacsaihuaman, the ruins of which can still be seen. Some of the individual stones in these walls weigh as much as twenty tons. Then, in the far background I could see the snow-clad summit of Mount Ausangate which rises to a height of nearly 21,000 feet.

My excursion to Tiahuanaco engraved a memory which I will never forget.

PART THREE

AFRICA and the SOUTH SEAS

Africa

I

THE LOST CITY OF THE SAHARA

Amid the snow-clad peaks of the high Atlas Mountains of Morocco there rises that strange river known as the Ziz, fated never to reach the sea, for after flowing southward for two hundred and fifty miles its waters die away in the thirsty desert sands. Midway along the course of this desert river, far out in the flat Sahara, is the great oasis of Tafilelt, and on the edge of the oasis are the remains of the city of Sijilmassa. Sijilmassa is truly the "Lost City" of North Africa, for though nowadays it consists of little more than acres of crumbling ruins stretching for two miles along the banks of the Ziz, formerly it was the capital of a Saharan empire ruled by kings whose power was felt from the Mediterranean to the Atlantic. But to-day Sijilmassa is better-known as a "City of the Dead", a sacred spot because there, in a mud-domed tomb, lies buried Mulai Reshed, the sultan who conquered Morocco in 1668.

Ever since the days of Musa ben Nasr, leader of the conquering Arabian horde, Europeans had striven in vain to reach the fabled "Kingdom of Tafilelt". Tales of the splendour of Sijilmassa, its capital, reached the Atlantic coastlands where the Portuguese conquistadors lay firmly entrenched in their stone castles, and sent them hastening off into the unknown desert. Whether or not they reached the old city history does not tell us; more probably they—like the Roman legions before them—were hurled back by the Berber fighting-men while crossing the Atlas Mountains.

Imperial Sijilmassa became one of the great cities of Africa, boasting a population of over a quarter of a million, for it controlled the caravan-road from the Niger to Tangier.

Though the city is reputed to have been patronized by Moorish and European merchants, it appears probable that these "Europeans" were really Moslem traders from the Near East. Its houses, palaces, castles, mosques and market-places were surrounded by great forests of date-palms, and along the highways which radiated from it in every direction camel caravans were continually arriving and departing.

In the seventeenth century Tafilelt became even more difficult of access for Christians, for now it was holy ground, the burial-place of Mulai Reshed the Conqueror. He led his cohorts over the Atlas Mountains, seized the throne of Morocco, and founded the dynasty which still survives to-day. Tafilelt was also a land of exile; it was the custom of the Moorish sultans to despatch thither their superfluous sons, who, being *shereefs* or descendants of the Prophet, fanatically repulsed European attempts to reach their city.

But enter it they eventually did. First to reach Sijilmassa was René Caillié, that dauntless son of a French baker, returning across the Sahara after being the first European to reach Timbuktu. This was in 1828; the oasis remained undisturbed until the arrival of Gerhard Rohlfs in 1864. These first explorers looked in vain for fabled Sijilmassa; the city was gone, destroyed by fire and sword, and only ruins remained. The first Englishman arrived in 1894 when Walter Harris, correspondent of *The Times*, travelled there in disguise from Marrakesh.

Then came the French conquest, and the beginnings of the pacification of southern Morocco. French troops fought their way over the mountains and established themselves in Tafilelt Oasis. But the fighting-men of the Sahara were in no mood to yield lightly. They rose and drove out the invaders and destroyed their fort. The French retired to the River Ziz and built there a new town called Erfoud. This was during the closing years of the First World War and the French had other things to think about than Saharan conquest.

Not until 1932 did the French return to Tafilelt and, after defeating the inhabitants of the oasis in a pitched battle, they re-built their fortress. Now the ruins of Sijilmassa were open to the world, or at least to those fortunate individuals who could secure sanction from the French military authorities to visit them. Such a journey I will now describe.

It has been said that beyond the High Atlas Mountains of Morocco, on the northern fringe of the Sahara, lies the most romantic and exotic land this side of Afghanistan. The world knows it simply as "The Zone of Insecurity", the territory but recently penetrated by the French. Powerful chieftains and hereditary saints still remain the despotic rulers of the country, dwelling in castles like feudal princes, surrounded by their retainers, slaves, and men-at-arms. Out amid the burning sands lie walled cities where ever-watchful riflemen guard the gates against the attacks of veiled raiders from the desert. If you would see Africa untamed, this is the place for you.

The road there is arduous, and not without danger. It is an old road, older than history, for it follows the route by which the caravans came from the Niger to Tangier. It sweeps south from the imperial city of Meknes, up and over the Middle Atlas Mountains, over the High Atlas Mountains, to Tafilelt. Its name now is the *Route Impériale*, the road of the French Foreign Legion, built by them to maintain their outposts in the desert. A few years ago caravans could only pass along it once every ten days, protected by armoured cars and flanking parties of friendly tribesmen.

South of Meknes we cross the invisible but potent line which divides "secure" from "insecure" Morocco, exchanging a land of comfort and safety for one where we are still liable to be killed on the spot to the greater glory of Allah. For Morocco is really divided into two parts. On the one hand we have the new Morocco created by the French, with its fine roads, hotels, schools and European-pattern towns, and on the other we have grim old Morocco, where men live according to a code which is absolutely alien to European thought and tradition.

As we travel southward along the road we realize that we are journeying into a land which belongs, not to our time, but to a time long past. We have stepped back into the medieval period of history, the colourful world of a thousand years ago, with all its romance and barbarity. Or perhaps it would be better to say that in Morocco the medieval and the modern exist side by side.

Before us the ten-thousand-foot barrier of the Middle Atlas Range rears its frowning peaks into the sky. Vast pine and cedar forests alternate with the burning, sun-scorched plains dotted with the black tents of the Berber nomads, where the salutation "I am the Guest of God" will procure hospitality. Forts crown the hills and men carry rifles as a matter of course. Arab tribesmen, on gaily caparisoned horses, ride swaggering past. We see their fortified villages clinging to the mountain sides, remote and inaccessible.

The people who live in this land are fierce and arrogant, hostile to Christians, but faithful to their own creed. Berbers, with or without a mixture of Arab blood, are a fighting race, and have always been "agin the government" whether it be Roman, Vandal, Arab or French. They fight for the love of it. Many of them are nomads, living in tents woven from the hair of goats and camels, while they move with their flocks and herds from one pasturage to another. Others live in fortified *ksour*, or villages of mud houses surrounded by walls and gates. Their methods of agriculture are simple, for they are content with little. In the spring they sow maize, beans and chick-peas; the autumn sowings provide them with barley.

Behind the first range of mountains lies another; the wall-like High Atlas towering up to over fourteen thousand feet appears impenetrable. You wonder how engineers ever contrived a way through—but they did; and a most amazing road it is. Through a series of terrific gorges, walled in by thousand-foot cliffs, defended by forts and machine-guns, the road of the French Foreign Legion winds its tortuous ways through the blood-red hills. This is Morocco's Khyber Pass: for thirty miles a continuous line of castles guard the passage.

At long last the mountains are left behind and we see before us for the first time the vast world of the Sahara stretching far away. French settlements appear at long inter-

A typical Lepcha from the Sikkim Himalayas

The Sikkim Himalayas, with Kinchinjunga in the distance

vals, rectangular blocks of red mud buildings, surrounded by crenellated walls and barbed-wire entanglements. If you were to visit one of these forts you might be surprised to discover that it contained a landing-field, radio station, electric light, tennis-courts and swimming-pool!

Beyond, one enters the valley of the Ziz, that strange river of canyons and castles. From the mushroom city of Erfoud it is only a dozen miles or so to Tafilelt and the ruins of Sijilmassa, but it took the French over a dozen years and a whole series of battles to cover those few miles. The Sahara stretches smooth and flat as far as the eye can see; then a green line shows up ahead, the outer fringe of the palm forests. Before you lies the red fortress of Rissani, with the tricolour floating over it, and yellow-turreted armoured cars standing in a line before the gate. Beyond lie the crumbling ruins of fabled Sijilmassa. This is the ancient kingdom of Tafilelt.

Though Tafilelt is no longer a separate kingdom it is still the largest oasis in Morocco, being some five hundred square miles in area, though in times of drought this area becomes considerably less. Though Sijilmassa is but a "City of the Dead", just acres of crumbling ruins beside the River Ziz, life continues in the oasis around it. Tafilelt possesses no less than a hundred and ten *ksour* or fortified villages which formerly warred continually among themselves.

It was to keep these war-like desert dwellers under control that Fort Rissani was built by Captain "Redcoat" de Bournazel, whose exploits are legendary in Morocco. Leader of the *Goums*, or native Berber cavalry, he received his name from the bright red tunic he wore when leading a charge. His general told him not to be so foolhardy and to wear khaki instead. De Bournazel obeyed, and on the first day he wore the new uniform, February 28, 1933, he was killed.

These *ksour* or mud houses in which now dwell all that is left of the population of ruined Sijilmassa, are one of the most astonishing forms of contemporary African architecture. Their high walls and gates and tapering towers have been variously attributed to the Egyptians, the Romans, and the Byzantines. They are usually square or oblong in shape

F   81

and reach a height of several storeys. Their resemblance to the "skyscraper" cities of the Hadramaut is striking, as can be seen by comparing the photographs of both.

In Tafilelt the old patriarchal mode of life prevails and were you to be invited inside one of these great mud strongholds by the *kaid* or sheik, you would sit cross-legged on a reed mat facing your host, while the sons of the house served you with glasses of mint tea poured from a gleaming samovar. Looking over the ramparts you would see the sheik's retainers drive the cattle into the courtyard for the night, and then take up their positions by the gate, on the lookout for possible marauders. It is a way of life which has hardly changed in a thousand years.

Outside the *ksour* would be the *nuadder* or threshing-floor. It is a wide circular platform of dried mud, upon which the grain is flung, and then trampled upon by horses driven round and round by sweating men and boys. Straw and chaff are thrown into the air, to be blown away by the wind, so that finally only the seed remains. The crops of barley, maize and millet are grown under the shelter of the palm trees.

Though the people of the oasis journey daily among the ruins of the great city which their ancestors built and dwelt in for hundreds of years, they can tell the traveller little about it. "It was there in our grandfathers' time", they will reply simply, a statement which may indicate a span of time as little as fifty years or more than a thousand. For this reason, it is always difficult to affix a date to African architecture.

An evasive reply is also characteristic of the native mind which suspects an ulterior motive in the precise statement of fact, and it is only when you have gained the confidence of the African that you will learn more. For among the present-day inhabitants there must be many whose grandparents could recall the destruction of Sijilmassa by the Arab tribe of the Ait Atta in 1818, and could describe how the old city, its walls breached and its gates down, witnessed the tumultous tribesmen pouring along its narrow streets, robbing, slaying and burning. So was Sijilmassa destroyed, and of the "pearl and pride of the Sahara" nothing now remains save vestiges of walls and towers, shapeless heaps of *tabia* or native concrete covered with vegetation, and a mosque in tolerably good condition.

There is one thing more, a legend of a golden treasure buried amid the ruins and guarded by *djinns* or demons. Now that the strong arm of France has brought peace once more to the land of Tafilelt who knows what archaeological excavation might not reveal among the ruins of this "lost city"? Here is an opportunity for someone to unravel a forgotten chapter of Saharan history.

2

PEOPLE OF THE VEIL

*N*owadays most people know that the old-fashioned idea of the Sahara, prevalent in our grandparents' time, as a vast desert of sand entirely devoid of life, is erroneous; they know instead that in the remote, sun-scorched interior of the Sahara are wide tracks of fertile country, high mountains with wooded valleys, and a native population which would not live anywhere else.

Among these Saharan tribes none is more interesting and fascinating than that strange race known as the Tuareg, or "People of the Veil", who live in the mountains of the central desert. Many romantic stories have been written of these tall, lean men who, mounted on camels, clothed in dark robes and veiled to the eyes, used to charge down on unsuspecting caravans with sword and lance. For untold generations it has been their custom to go pillaging and raiding. "The Forgotten of God" is the name by which this battle-hungry race is known among neighbouring tribes.

For centuries there has been considerable speculation concerning the origin of the Tuareg, some writers considering them to be the descendants of the Vandals who conquered North Africa in the fifth century, while others declare them to be descended from Crusaders who became lost in the desert and never returned home. Whatever truth there may be in these stories there is certainly much that is curious and puzzling about the Tuareg. What is the origin of the veil which the men (instead of the women, as is usual in Moslem countries), wear? How did they get their double-edged swords of Crusader type? Why are they the only Berber race to possess a written language?

To reach the country occupied by the Tuareg you have to travel a thousand miles due south of Algiers to the great mountain massifs of Hoggar, Ajser and Air. Few races on earth can possess such a vast expanse of territory in which to dwell as the Tuareg, for they occupy a million and a half square miles of the Sahara, or about half the area of the United States. Their homelan dconstitutes one of the most desolate and inaccessible terrains on earth, which before the days of motor and air transport was almost impossible to reach. Its landscape is mainly one of sandy deserts, stony deserts, dried-up river-beds, and mountain ranges with granite peaks over two miles high.

Across this vast domain the Tuareg lead the life of no-madic herdsmen, living in tents made of goat-skins. A cur-tain divides the tent into two apartments: one for the man, where his weapons and saddle are kept, the other for the woman. The Tuareg encampments are small and widely dispersed, for the arid countryside is not capable of support-ing a large population; indeed, the population of the whole Sahara is vastly inferior in numbers to many an English town.

The greatest peculiarity of the Tuareg is that all the men veil their faces with a dark-blue or white strip of thin cloth called a *tagilmus*, about six feet long and eight inches wide. It is wrapped round the head to form a hood over the eyes, called *teineder*, and a covering over the mouth and nose. Hence the Tuareg are known as the *Kel Tagilmus*, the "People of the Veil". The men never unveil, considering it almost indecent to do so. The women, on the other hand, are not veiled. Actually the Tuareg never call themselves by this name, which is Arabic in origin, but style themselves *Imouhar*, "The Noble Ones".

Another peculiarity of the Tuareg is their caste system, for they are divided into a noble class, a worker class, and a slave class. The noble class has to provide the leaders and chief fighting-men; the worker class has to serve as their vassals, and pay tribute and provide fighting-men when called upon to do so. At the head of the system is the *amenokal*, king, or sultan, a hereditary title which descends, not from father to son, but to the eldest son of the king's eldest sister, for they are a matriarchal people.

Tuareg nobles consider it disgraceful to work for a living, and are supported by their vassals and slaves. "May shame overwhelm the family that tills the soil", is their maxim, and formerly their lives were spent in fighting and raiding other tribes. Since the final conquest of the Sahara by the French such raids are no longer possible, for French troops police the Sahara and quickly punish law-breakers. Consequently the Tuareg nobles find themselves with no purpose in life, apart from looking after their camels.

Without the camel, life in the middle of the Sahara would not be possible, for the movements of the tribes are regulated by their constant search for water and pasturage for their herds. The camel can live and thrive where no other beast of burden can find subsistence, and carry loads across shifting sands impossible to wheeled vehicles. The camel's hair can be made into wool for the manufacture of tents and clothing, and its flesh and milk form a great part of the desert dweller's food supply. To the Arab the camel is truly indispensable.

Among the Tuareg, women hold a most honoured position. They enjoy great freedom before marriage, and are notorious for the number of love affairs they indulge in. At each encampment a special tent is erected, away from the others, where the young men and girls can indulge in lovemaking. In this way many an agreeable evening is spent in the desert. But though they are broad-minded in sexual matters the Tuaregs are strict to maintain the social barriers between the castes, and a woman who takes a lover of inferior birth is ostracized.

Tuareg women are very independent, and can divorce their husbands when they wish. It is often the woman who proposes to the man, and she will often travel long distances to be with her lover. Women of the noble class do not work, for even such occupations as knitting and weaving are considered degrading. They spend their time looking after their children and in gossiping. The women play the chief part in family affairs. They advise the men, and it is rare for the latter not to listen, and take their advice. A French officer with whom I travelled in the Sahara told me that a short time previously a deputation of Tuareg women had complained to him that when he had to discuss important matters relating to the tribe he summoned the Tuareg men, but not the women.

"Our law is different from yours," explained the buxom matron who acted as leader of the deputation. "Here in the desert it is we women who give the orders, and the men who obey. It is our ancient law."

One does not need to sojourn at a Tuareg encampment for very long to realize that their society is based on matriarchal principles. F. R. Rodd in his book *The People of the Veil*, tells of his conversation with a Tuareg: "This man, to emphasize the good manners required by usage to be observed before women, assured me that in the old days if anyone had dared to break wind in their presence, the insult was punishable by death alone." This suggests an almost incredibly high standard of manners for primitive tent dwellers.

Tuareg women, in their blue robes, sometimes embellished with rough silver jewellery, look anything but glamorous pin-up girls, for their hard life amid the burning desert sands makes them appear old and wizened, though they may be hardly thirty years of age. Incidentally, the make-up used by amorous maidens would scare away any but the most ardent suitors, for it consists of painting the face with red and yellow ochre. As they very rarely—if ever—wash, their bodies become stained with the blue dye from their clothing.

Although the Tuareg are nominally Moslems they observe few Moslem customs, and the more orthodox Arabs regard them as savages. There is nothing in common between the Tuareg and the Arabs, either in racial type, language, way of life, temperament or character. Compared with the Arab, the Tuareg is a simpler, harder, and less subtle type of being. The Arab is accustomed to regard anything which may happen to him, especially a misfortune, as *Kismet* or God's will, but the Tuareg temperament is not one to bow submissively to any power. The Tuareg is accustomed to looking out across the Sahara not as an underling but as a master.

At present the Tuareg's propensity to go raiding every now and then proves too strong in spite of the French troops: a caravan is raided and a few men die. The Tuareg have proved awkward customers to deal with in two world wars, and may prove even more awkward in the future.

* * *

Come with me to one of the camps of the Tuareg, at Tamanraset, in the Hoggar Mountains. Here, where the great peaks tower up eight and nine thousand feet, is the "capital" of the *Amenokal*, or King of the Hoggar Tuareg. They are waiting for us—a circle of tall men, dressed in long, black robes, their faces veiled so that only their dark eyes are visible. With their big camel-hide shields, slender lances and long straight swords they make an impressive picture. Behind them is a circle of black camel-skin tents.

Into one of these tents, when greetings are over, we will be invited. It is a long low structure, little more than five feet in height, with a few skins and rugs on the floor, a few cushions and boxes to serve as furniture. Slaves bring in cups of tea on a brass tray, but this is only the prelude to the meal which follows: a sheep, roasted whole, and *cous-cous*, a favourite dish made of broken grains of wheat mixed with meat and vegetables. No knives and forks are used. The roast meat is eaten by tearing off lumps of flesh and stuffing them into your mouth, the *cous-cous* by rolling some of the hot, sticky mess into a ball between fingers and thumb and tossing it neatly into your mouth. Your host may honour you by picking some delicacy out of the pot and sticking it in your mouth, a sheep's eye, for instance. You cannot refuse, for the tribesmen will stare at you and wonder why you are so ill-mannered. Taureg live simply; and seldom eat meat.

Later there will be an entertainment, perhaps a camel dance or a sham battle. The former is a very curious spectacle, for while the women sit around and produce peculiar music on drums and pipes the men manoeuvre their camels round and round, in and out, in intricate movements, keeping time to the music. The gyrations of the big beasts and their riders are a very odd "dance" indeed.

More exciting is a sham Tuareg battle. Looking towards the horizon you see two lines of camels approaching, one from either side of the camp, armed men on their backs. They charge down upon the tents, and when it seems almost impossible for them to avoid knocking these over, the beasts are reined in so suddenly that the sand rises about them in drifting clouds. When this happens you probably breathe a sigh of relief, having visualized yourself being ridden down by one of the huge beasts.

More excitement follows, as the two groups of riders spring to the ground, hurling their lances at each other. Nobody seems to be hurt, however, so they take hold of their long swords and attack each other fiercely. A dozen individual hand-to-hand combats now take place simultaneously, with the swordsmen dodging in and out like fighting cocks. They leap backwards and forwards and sideways, and you hear the thud-thud of the sword blades on the big camel-hide shields, and catch the flash of sunlight on metal. But although there is plenty of noise and shouting, not much damage is done, except when a man gets excited and, forgetting that it is only a game, slashes an opponent to the bone. Eventually it all ends as suddenly as it began, and the combatants troop off to have a drink.

Few scenes I have witnessed proved as thrilling as that mock Taureg battle.

From real battles to mock battles! Thus have the destinies of the Tuareg changed within the last fifty years. The beginning of this century saw them regarded as almost supernatural beings, raiders before whom all the peoples of the Sahara cringed, a race numerically small, but one which enjoyed a world-wide notoriety and prestige. Now that reputation has vanished; and though they may occasionally plunder and slay, they have to procure the things they need by buying them, as do the other tribes administered by the French. For the internal combustion engine, in the shape of the aeroplane and the armoured car, opened up the interior of the Sahara to the white man's deadly armament. It took petrol to conquer the Tuareg.

But they are still one of the oddest races existing!

3

ZIMBABWE—CITY OF GOLD

In the case of many ruined cities we now know quite a lot about them, about their origin and the people who lived in them. But one dead city still provides endless speculation as to its history. I refer to Zimbabwe.

Who built this city and when? For what reason have these mysterious ruins not yet given up their secret? Why, indeed, should there have existed this great metropolis in the centre of Africa, remote from any other civilization? No bones have yet been found, only some gold, some pottery and some good stone sculptures.

Certain experts maintain that these are thousands of years old. A lady archaeologist who only a few years ago was engaged by the Southern Rhodesian Government to go into the matter declared that they were Bantu and of about the fourteenth or fifteenth century A.D.. Yet a Portuguese wrote in the sixteenth century that he had heard of them, and that they were then already very old. Even the Queen of Sheba is dragged in, the Land of Ophir, and the Phoenicians.

It is well known that Zimbabwe provided the description for Rider Haggard's *She*. Writers, archaeologists, historians, all find in Zimbabwe a challenge to their imagination. Certainly every visitor is invariably deeply stirred by what can be seen there and over which hangs a veil of profoundest mystery. Many thousands of visitors from the Union of South Africa and from other countries come to see the ruins every year. There is good hotel accommodation locally, and the place is a popular holiday camping-ground with Rhodesians.

The Zimbabwe Ruins lie about seventeen miles south of Fort Victoria, that small township whose origin began with the building of a fort by the pioneers, about sixty years ago, to withstand the natives in the Matabele Rebellion.

The surrounding scenery is impressively grand and romantic. Rugged hills of fantastic shape, long lines of tall cliffs, gorges and caves and tall finger-rocks are the most prominent features. Scattered around, rather sparsely, are a number of native villages, and from these at night one often hears the tom-toms, giving out their weird, monotonous music—a music which tugs at one's heart-strings and arouses nostalgic memories when one is far away from it.

The Zimbabwe Ruins were discovered in 1868 by Adam Renders, a wandering American hunter and trader. He stumbled across them one day on his travels, and found them buried in deep tropical foliage and undergrowth. It proved to be a momentous discovery although the importance of his find was probably hidden from him, because it was impossible to examine the ruins closely owing to the dense growth of vegetation. On further examination they were found to be in a marvellous state of preservation and of remarkable workmanship. The name "Zimbabwe" is of local native origin, meaning "the buildings of stones", but there are no native legends to account for the origin of what was once a vast city.

That Zimbabwe is situated in the heart of a gold-bearing mountainous region, gives rise to the popular belief that in this neighbourhood was an ancient Witwatersrand, and that this area had to be protected against possible enemies. Scattered all over Southern Rhodesia are the remains of ancient ruins and of workings, from which, according to experts, £150,000,000 to £200,000,000 worth of gold was removed.

The most important building still standing is the Elliptical Temple. Its walls average from 22 to 32 feet in height, are wide at the base and narrowed on the summit. The thickest walls are fifteen feet wide at the base and ten feet at the summit. This lean-back of the sides of the walls lends to the building a most striking appearance. The total length of the passage-ways within the temple is 360 feet; while the circumference of the exterior is 830 feet.

No single one of the many hundreds of ruins of the oldest type in Southern Rhodesia gives any sign of ever having possessed a roof. At the Temple—the most intact and best-preserved of these structures—there are absolutely no evidences of it ever having been roofed. The very large area enclosed, the irregular size, and various other factors, all tend to exclude any suggestion that once it may have had a roof. If this Temple was formerly, as most experts agree, a place where Phallic worship, even in a degenerate form, was practised, then it would not have been roofed over. It is a matter of knowledge that light, sunlight, was regarded as symbolic of Phallic worship. The sun engenders the fruitfulness of the earth, and so became an emblem of the nature worship of ancient days, being represented by symbols of the generative power similar to those once carried in the Bacchic processions of the Greeks. The interior conical towers—the large one representing the male generative power and the small one that of the female—correspond to the Sacred Cone in the ruins at the Phoenician Temple at Byblos.

There are four entrances to this temple, with apparently no gates or doors, and inside are remnants of walls and passages straggling in several directions. Obviously they must have served some specific purpose. Perhaps they formed a kind of maze which made the journey of worshippers to the holy of holies more mysterious. Possibly, too, some were used by the priests as behind-the-scenes approaches to the centres of ceremonies. Incidentally, no cement or mortar has been used in any of the construction, but there are efficient methods of drainage, both indicating that the theory of Bantu origin is most unlikely.

A feature of the exterior wall is the chevron pattern which runs along it near the top. The chevron is one of the oldest decorative patterns known. It is found plentifully on all ancient Egyptian buildings and on Phoenician coins, also it is quite commonly used by the present-day African peoples. It is the ancient hieroglyphic for water, as well as being the Zodiacal sign of Aquarius. It was the symbol of fertility, and this probably accounts for its presence in this temple. It is noteworthy that the pattern is laid, throughout its entire length, on an exact level. It is worked out in granite blocks, and it appears in relief owing to the interstices of the pattern being filled in with granite slabs not brought flush to the face of the pattern.

Between the Elliptical Temple and the Acropolis on the nearby Zimbabwe Hill is the Valley of the Ruins. Here is a conglomeration of ruins in scattered heaps, and these still await more thorough investigation. Some of them are massive and well-built, and are undoubtedly antique: others are of poor construction and obviously of a much later period. In the older ruins have been discovered relics which indicate a considerable age, but in the poorer buildings nothing has yet been found relating to any period prior to the twelfth or thirteenth century A.D.

There appears to be no set plan in their construction or design other than the purpose either of residential quarters for the former inhabitants of Zimbabwe, or of defences connected with the Temple and the Acropolis. The fact that the Valley abounds in ruins of all types and ages, extending over an area of several square miles, indicates that at one time there must have existed a city of considerable size and housing a great population.

Towering majestically above the surrounding country and looking down on the Elliptical Temple and the Valley of the Ruins, the Zimbabwe Hill's summit is crowned by one of the most interesting ruins in the African continent. Apart from archaeological and architectural considerations, the Acropolis on Zimbabwe Hill offers the student of military engineering and strategy a wide field for investigation.

On many occasions I have climbed to the top of the cyclopean mountain, 200–300 feet high (for some years I lived not far distant from Zimbabwe), through the steep and narrow cleft between two immense and smooth rocks by a passage one man could easily defend against a host of enemies. And as I observed the tremendously steep and strong fortress walls surmounted by a number of stone steles, ending in an archaic eagle or buzzard keeping watch over this stronghold, one idea and fact kept impressing itself on me—that this mountain was and is a stronghold, impregnable if defenders are sufficiently provided with water and food.

It must have been the Keep, the last refuge and also the dwelling-place of the ruler over Zimbabwe, from which he could look down over his city. I remember on one occasion when I was looking down from this eyrie I saw to my horror that my small camp, just below the temple walls, was being investigated by some wild pigs searching for food. I raced down the hill in record time to disperse the animals. Unfortunately they had already done some damage.

I remember, too, as I lay out under the stars at night I tried to force my imagination to call up the ghosts of the distant past; but I was not successful. On occasion, elsewhere, I have succeeded in recreating vividly the ancient past, especially on moonlit nights: notably at Angkor and Pompeii.

The summit of Zimbabwe Hill is about 350 feet above the surrounding country and dominates it for many miles. The hill is an isolated one, and in general appearance is a rugged granite kopje clothed with masses of trees and vegetation all up its steep slopes. It is faced by sheer cliffs of great height, which render it inaccessible on three sides, and most difficult of ascent on the fourth.

This stronghold provided by Nature was artificially strengthened by the erection of massive ramparts, traverses, screen-walls, intricate entrances, narrow and labyrinthine passages, sunken thoroughfares, banquette walls, parapets, and other devices of a people who were intimately conversant with military engineering and defensive tactics. In their very ingenuity of construction and design, their massive character, and the persistent repetition at every single point of vantage, these defences cannot fail to astonish even the greatest experts in military engineering. Those who know the minds and ways of the Bantu people realize that a far more intelligent brain designed the Acropolis than any possessed by the present natives of Africa. It is true that, at later periods, they have profited by such an expert example of fortifications, but only in a very crude and degenerate form.

Nature here offered the original builders the best of all possible sites on which to apply their ingenuity. This they achieved in an astounding manner. Only a sudden surprise attack, launched possibly when the defenders were weakened or incapacitated by debauchery or religious orgies, could have carried that wonderful stronghold.

Above the precipices, as seen from the valley below, are massive walls; and on the summits of these are monoliths, still more or less erect, standing clear-cut against the sky-line. Viewed from this point alone—and it represents only a small fraction of the walls of which the Acropolis is composed—it is possible to realize that many thousands of tons of granite blocks must have been transported up the sides of that precipitous hill to a height of close on 300 feet. Examination of the rocks on the Zimbabwe Hill prove conclusively that by far the greater quantity of stone employed in the construction of the walls was neither quarried on nor anywhere near the hill itself. This is a matter which has been proved beyond all question.

Apart from the infinite patience and painstaking toil displayed in the methods of construction to complete the rather complicated plans for this stronghold, the fact that so much weighty stone was carried up to such a height, which a man unburdened can climb only with difficulty, is one to perplex and amaze the most casual observer. To those with some knowledge of military engineering, the contemplation of these works is most profitable.

How did all this civilization come to an end? The assumption must be that the inhabitants were annihilated suddenly by some barbarous race, for there are undoubted evidences of hasty departure shown both at the ruins and at the ancient gold mines in the neighbourhood. Gold ornaments have been discovered, and these were broken or damaged as if in the course of a mighty struggle. Apparently the defenders of Zimbabwe were given no chance to remove their hoards of wealth. It is highly probable that they were the victims of an overwhelming force of Bantu people, who arrived suddenly from the north.

A Swiss antiquarian, Mr. Raoul Gerard, a recent investigator at Zimbabwe, puts forward a novel theory. He turns down any idea that the city was built by the Bantus themselves and on their own inspiration. He mentions in his report that when the Spaniards in 1519 went to Mexico, the Aztecs told them of Tonatiu, the Sun-God, who in ancient times came, with red-golden hair, blue eyes and a white skin, and ruled wisely over them as a beneficial god. In fact, they believed red-haired and laughing Alvarado to be Tonatiu come back. In all probability, claims Mr. Gerard, Tonatiu was a Viking thrown on the shores of Central America, and Alvarado a descendant of the blonde Visigoths or Vandals who went to Spain.

Bearing this in mind, the hypothesis takes shape that in days gone by one or more white people came to Zimbabwe from the Mediterranean, Babylonia, India, or even China, were accepted as wise rulers by the Bantu tribes, and imposed on them their higher civilization, some remnants of which are the existing stone sculptures with a frieze of bulls, and those impressive stone birds keeping watch on the fortress walls and now dispersed in various museums. This theory has as much chance of being correct as any of the many others. Most people, however, may wish that the riddle of Zimbabwe may never be solved; since it is much more interesting to speculate about its past.

General view of the Zimbabwe ruins, showing the Elliptical Temple

One of the conical towers within the Elliptical Temple

The Acropolis, Zimbabwe

4

THE WEB-FOOTED

This is not a chapter about ducks, but about the Batwa, concerning whom I made mention in the introductory chapter. These swamp-dwellers are the most primitive, the least known, and quite the strangest people that inhabit Northern Rhodesia.

They are found in at least three different parts of the country, hundreds of miles apart—in the Bangweulu swamps (where I once came upon them when making a cycle trip to the grave of Livingstone's heart at Chitambo), in the Lukanga swamp, and on the Kafue Flats, which are swamps, too, for about seven months in every year.

The Batwas have chiefs of a sort, and tribal law, adhered to more or less. Gradually they are being civilized, but the process is not easy. Not so many years ago their homes were just little reed shelters built on floating platforms in the swamps. Their diet consisted of fish and water-lily roots. They seldom ventured on dry land, and then only to do essential trading. But even in their commerce they were always most careful not to encounter anybody. They brought their fish by night and laid it down at the foot of some big tree or by the side of a well-worn track. The next morning their native neighbours came along with maize and salt and left some there in exchange for the fish, which they then carried away with them. The following night along came the Batwa again, creeping out from the reeds in their small canoes, and took what they found home to their expectant families.

One wonders how this strange form of trading started. Its peculiar form must obviously have been due to an inherited fear handed down from generation to generation. Nowadays, however, the Batwa have lost this fear-complex, for they appreciate that our rule spells safety to them. Yet, I have often heard other natives in this part of Africa refer to the Batwa with the utmost contempt. "Batwa!" they exclaim. "They live on the eggs of crocodiles and have skin between their toes like *Chivuwe* the goose!"

For many years the collection of hut taxes by the Northern Rhodesia Government was a problem, but the local District Officers have now got the matter pretty well tied-up. The necessity for finding the cash required for taxation has even brought some of the younger Batwa away from their homes in search of work. In a country where the annual tax is still only a matter of shillings per head, it does not take long to earn the money; but contact with civilization soon sows the seeds of desire for others things.

It was some years ago that I accompanied a District Officer, a friend of mine, who had decided that he wished to visit some of his Batwa charges. It was the dry season when we set out, accompanied by bearers, over the vast and, at that time, dry Kafue Flats. Our route took us along beside the River Kafue, which meanders over the never-ending plain.

It was early spring, the sun was hot, and the going was rough. I can still recollect the unpleasantness of some of our trek: how we stumbled over tussock grass, half-blind with sweat, the large ground cracks and the ant-bear holes which had to be carefully avoided on pain of incurring a sprained ankle. We cursed (*how* we cursed!) and we were almost weeping with frustration and discomfort on the last lap of our approach to a remote Batwa village.

When we did at last attain our goal, it was to find ourselves in a horrible, nauseating spot. It stank of rotting fish which were spread out on the roofs to dry. Then there were the flies—millions of them—but the only signs of life were one naked baby with sore eyes and a long brown dog that was a slinking skeleton.

The District Officer told one of his police "boys" to go and find the local residents; and, in the meantime, we tried to escape the worst of the odour by getting to a spot that was well up-wind. We could hear sounds of life in the village, partly due to the native policeman rousing the Batwa from their afternoon *siesta*. After a few minutes an agitated old man was brought before us. He was dressed in a long blue cloth and a necklace of white shells. His hair was done up in a cone behind. This was the village headman.

But the D.O. wanted to meet all the villagers. To collect them before us led to a further long delay. At last, however, they were prodded by the police to where we were standing near an ant-hill, and clapped "Good-day". Never in my life have I seen such miserable creatures (excepting a prison camp I visited in Germany in 1945). The headman was the only one who possessed a whole garment of any sort other than a loin-cloth. One or two of the younger men had strung about their middles what once might have been a pair of shorts. These only served to emphasize their nudity. The majority had only narrow strips of game-skin. The women had kilts of the same material; in most cases they were covered modestly to their knees.

It was not their clothing which struck one so much as their physique and woe-begone expressions. Their bodies were of a revolting shape, worse even than the repulsive effigies of Bushmen to be seen in the Cape Town Museum. Their feet were large, their legs short and thin, their posteriors and stomachs remarkably protuberant, their arms long, their heads large, their shoulders heavy. They had sloping foreheads, flat noses, thick lips and massive jaws, black with woolly whiskers that had never been cut or shaved. They looked like human apes. It seemed hard, as I studied this little gathering, as primitive as any I have ever encountered, to imagine that they could ever have had any history. The wonder, in fact, is how they have ever survived through the ages. Yet the Batwa have their own heroic story. It is one of the most astonishing things about them. Once they fought and conquered, and their leader was a warrior queen who died of a broken heart.

It was the D.O., a remarkably fine native linguist and a man of great sympathy, who, with considerable difficulty, extracted the story from the dead queen's son, the old headman who now squatted before us, and it was confirmed by another old man of the village. As the epic was gradually pieced together I found it difficult to picture the Batwa as ever having been brave men; but I changed my mind later when I learned that even now they do not hesitate to tackle a wounded buffalo single-handed with a spear.

This, then, is the story of a Batwa Boadicea.

It must have been in the eighteen-nineties—a time when what is now Northern Rhodesia knew little of the white man. At that time there was still much fighting going on between the various native tribes. In particular the Baila were great fighters. Even the great Barotse nation found it hard to resist their raids, and if only the Baila had not indulged in internal quarrels, the latter could never have conquered them.

It was when the Barotse sent an army down the Kafue to try and conquer the Batonga that they found the Batwa barred the way. Still, the Barotse were in overwhelming force and their reputation was frightening. In consequence, the Batwa fled eastward to the Batonga country.

The Batwa then, as now, "have no legs", as their neighbours say. They had spent their lives in canoes, and they arrived at the top of the watershed, footsore, dispirited and terrified. There they halted, for beyond them lay no sanctuary, only the tumbled hills of the escarpment falling to the Zambezi.

I know that country, and can well picture the wretched position of the Batwas. Around is a welter of arid mountains and stony precipices. The only trees are so stunted that they provide no shelter from the fierce rays of the sun. A cooling breeze is a rarity in this sun-baked land. There are practically no villages, and even fewer livestock.

It was here on the highest ridge—and the place was later called Manpagazia ("the stones of blood")—that the Batwa stood. They could not face those hills. The Barotse must have been tired too. They had marched three hundred miles, and they were a people of the plains, used to sand.

No one will ever know how the battle went on that high grassy ridge, whether the slaughter did indeed make the stones run red with blood, or whether, as so often happened in Africa, after a lot of harmless spear-throwing, the invaders were seized with sudden, groundless panic and fled. All that remains is the undoubted story of this African queen with her web-footed warriors driving the Barotse back to the borders of their own country, many, many miles away.

This, then, was the epic of the Batwa; although I doubt whether it still holds any place among the modern members of this tribe. The epic ended in tragedy, for the gallant queen who had led them so well to victory failed later to make her Batwa into a people. My epilogue tell of how this woman was to die of a broken heart.

Following this battle, the queen, free now from outside interference, did her best to make her subjects happy. For many years they lived happily and undisturbed. The white man came: the administration, railways, traders. The last-named, as usual, were the first to arrive in the Batwa country. There was one pioneer trader who initiated the queen into the mysteries of money. He told her how useful it would be when the white man's government came along to demand a hut tax. He suggested that she should send her young men to work for him, so that this shining silver could be obtained. She agreed. The young men worked, bringing to her handfuls of coins.

Shortly afterwards there came a government official to discuss the matter of hut tax. Proudly the old queen displayed her pile of silver coins. Imagine her horror when the white man looked at the coins and said they would not do! The trader had been palming off on his Batwa labourers Portuguese money. The official refused to accept this, and told her that she must produce British currency when he next called.

The problem of how to raise this money was insoluble. When the tax collector returned some months later it was to find the queen sitting alone outside her hut. All her subjects had fled in their canoes into the swamps, taking their few possessions with them. They had forsaken her. All was finished. She could fight no more.

The collector burned down every hut except hers, and

went away. Probably he intended to teach these Batwa, once and for all, a lesson and a respect for the administration and the law.

A night or two later the Batwa returned to their burned-down village. Doubtless they were ashamed of what they had done, when they found their queen sitting outside her hut—dead.

South Seas

A MYSTERY OF THE SOUTH SEAS

As a general rule one would hardly look for the ruins of a great city on a remote island in the South Seas, and it is this fact which renders the oft-described but little visited "Ruins of Ponape" of even more interest. For the creation of a city implies a fairly high degree of civilization, a substantial background of history, and a stable government with powers over a fairly wide radius of territory. These are not qualities which one usually associates with the islands of the South Seas which, until the coming of the white men, were lands without history, in a primitive stage of culture, peopled by natives, Polynesian or Melanesian peoples, engrossed in warfare and cannibalism. One would not look to such people for the creation of great fortresses, temples and palaces, all built of enduring stone to last for centuries.

Yet on the small island of Ponape, in the Caroline Islands, a thousand miles from the mainland of China or Australia, is the ruined city of Nan Matal, which very appropriately has been called "The Venice of the South Seas" for here, erected in the waters of a shallow lagoon, are over ninety majestic buildings, of a type which cannot be found in any other part of the globe. Even in ruins the city is still of considerable beauty, a wonder to all who see it. As one passes along the canals (now filled in with sand) which serve as streets, stone buildings which once housed kings, nobles and priests tower up on either side. Yet no one knows who built these gigantic ruins, or how old they are, for Nan Matal is still one of the most mysterious places in the world.

Ponape is the largest of the Caroline Islands, whose area of about three hundred and forty square miles is covered with mountains which nowhere rise much above two thousand feet. (Ponape itself rises to three thousand feet.) The mountains are densely wooded, and tangled vegetation covers the great masses of eroded basalt of which most of the island is composed, so that travelling is difficult. Much of the interior is covered with swamps—a desolate, inhospitable place. Most of the population of about nine thousand live in settlements along the coast: copra is produced in large quantities.

It is known that formerly the island was divided into five states, the most powerful of which was known as Matolenim, which means "the space between the houses". Nan Matal was the residence of the kings of Matolenim, and their attendant priests and nobles. The name Ponape means "on the stones", i.e., the holy stones, for the city was regarded as sacred.

The city was divided into three parts; the lower town which was the home of the king; the upper town, the residence of the priests; and the walls which surrounded both these places and which were utilized as burying-places for the dead. Tombs, vaults and mausoleums were built into the walls. All the buildings were regarded as holy, for the town was taboo to the common people and only chiefs and priests had admittance. It was certain death for the ordinary people to come inside, though exceptions were made at the celebration of certain religious ceremonies.

The ruins are not easy of access, for most of them are covered by a dense growth of trees and bushes, so that only glimpses of walls and buildings are visible. Blocks of basalt or coral, appearing grey or red in hue because of the moss which covers them, can be seen through the dark green foliage as you pass along the waterways which divide the buildings. But enough remains to give a good impression of the appearance of the principal buildings of the town at the height of their splendour.

For Nan Matal is very likely a dead city of comparatively recent origin. Less than a hundred years ago it was inhabited by a prosperous and contented people, but the arrival of over-zealous Christian missionaries resulted in the population leaving their homes and abandoning the city for the jungle. Some buildings which were in the course of construction were left unfinished, and the grandeur of Nan Matol became a thing of the past.

Various travellers visited the site—Gulick, the American missionary, J. S. Kubary the German, the English traveller F. W. Christian—and produced the first maps of the "Holy Stones", but by then the worship of the sacred turtle and other pagan gods was forgotten, and Nan Matal was already a city of legend. It was not until 1908–10 that Dr. Paul Hambruch, of the Ethnological Museum, Hamburg, surveyed adequately the ruined city, mapping the separate buildings and providing an explanation of their function.

It gives one a curious sensation to follow the waterways of this abandoned city, and to try and visualize something of the life of the race which built it. Though the origin of the city is shrouded in mystery, the names of a few personages connected with events which took place there before the jungle overwhelmed it are known, though very inadequately. What sort of man, for instance, was Iso Kalakal, the conqueror of Ponape, whose tomb is the only building standing on dry land? That he was a person with a considerable knowledge of ballistics is shown by the mound of big ovoid sling-stones piled inside one of the buildings.

What sort of man, also, was Sau Telur, the last king of Ponape? There is a building known as Kalapuel, "The Place of Strangers", where Iso Kalakal received the king's hospitality, and where the quarrel took place in which Sau Telur lost his life and crown. These two shadowy figures intrigue us, as we are intrigued by the even more shadowy figures which founded the city several centuries before. For who built Nan Matal? We do not know, and it is difficult even to hazard a guess. It might have been Neolithic men. It might have been a party of Spanish colonists centuries ago, bound for some place in the Indies and blown far off their course. It might have been Japanese settlers in medieval times. It might have been a race preceding the present one. Yet Dr. Hambruch would have none of this. The buildings were not constructed by the Spaniards, nor have they anything to do with similar buildings in Japan. According to him they are not more than two or three centuries old, and were the work of the native population. Yet the problem persists: if this work was not directed by some conqueror from across the sea, then some person locally must have possessed considerable technical knowledge.

Among the principal buildings which one encounters on a tour of the ruins is the temple-palace known as the Pan-Katara. Formerly it was the seat of the king, who was looked upon as a god; the place was also the temple of Nan Japue, the principal Ponapean god, and here sacrifices to the sacred turtle took place. Another great building is Nan Tauas, a mausoleum of the dead, where in four big vaults the kings and nobles were laid to rest; burials also took place on top of the walls and in the galleries built inside them. There they rest, the accumulated dead of several centuries, tier upon tier, still within sound of the sea which formed the background to their lives when they worked and loved in this ruined city so many generations ago.

For, as befits a people who lived almost on the sea, one can still see much that entered into the fabric of their lives; their bathing places, and the sites where they held their sports, their canoe races and the like. One can see their cooking places, and the deep holes where they fished for oysters and other shellfish. One can see the pool where the sacred eel was kept and fed on the flesh of turtles which were cooked in the little building alongside. Here is a place where a chief, having been offended by another chief, burnt himself and his tribe rather than be shamed. But of the people themselves, only mouldering bones and a few legends are left.

Beyond that there is for contemplation nothing but the gigantic buildings which they raised, the construction of which is still a source of wonder. Great walls 6 feet thick and nearly 30 feet high, confront the traveller; doorways with lintels made from basalt slabs over 20 feet long. Basalt and coral-stone were the principal materials used in the construction of the buildings. The basalt was probably floated to the site on large rafts, after having been quarried on the neighbouring states of Ú, Nantiati and Lot, in the south of the island.

We do not know why it was decided to built the city in a shallow lagoon between two islands. Once a site on the reefs had been selected a group of artificial islands was constructed, large four-sided platforms on which the buildings were erected. To make these artificial islands large blocks of basalt were laid in the shallow water, four to six feet apart, and the space between them was filled in with loose stones. On top of the first layer a second layer of basalt blocks was laid crosswise, then alternate layers until the required height was reached; this was usually about nine feet.

The houses, palaces and temples were built on top of the platforms, surrounded by walls from ten to thirty feet high. They were built in the same fashion, of alternate layers of basalt laid at right angles, and the spaces in between filled with smaller layers of stone. The corners were further strengthened by little square towers. The basalt was mostly used in the form of long columns, or in large round blocks. These often weighed several tons, and were hauled into position by means of levers, and by using large tree trunks as inclined planes.

The whole undertaking presupposes an extensive labour force, and a stable government directed by some person possessed of considerable engineering ability. Even then the building of the city must have required hard work on the part of several generations of Ponapeans. But who they were, and how they became possessed of the urge to raise such a memorial to their race, we cannot say. Yet there, a thousand miles and more from any sources of civilized knowledge, the lost city of Nan Matal still stands!

THE SECRET VALLEY

The widespread use of aircraft during the Second World War led to the opening up of many hitherto inaccessible regions of the globe. Areas which had formerly defied exploration and remained a mystery to the outside world now became comparatively familiar to the men who made regular service flights across them. So many interesting and unusual discoveries were made that the science of exploration underwent rapid development, but owing to the necessity for secrecy, many of the discoveries could not be made public at the time. Most of the exploration of the future will be to follow up discoveries made during the war years.

In no other country in the world are there more possibilities of future development than in the great island of New Guinea. It is the largest island in the world (after Greenland and the island-continent of Australia), and although it had been known to Europeans for several centuries, even at the outbreak of war in 1939 much of it was unexplored. A tropical country covered with jungle, it was known to possess mountains high enough to be covered with glaciers. The settled areas produced rubber, cotton, cacao, coconuts and sisal. Aircraft flights to newly-discovered goldfields were opening up parts of the interior.

Allied servicemen, sent to New Guinea to fight the Japanese, found themselves living for months at a time in areas completely unknown to Europeans. A party of Australian troops, patrolling the Milne Bay area, reported the existence of a strange tribe of pygmies known as the Moikodis. The average height of these people was three feet. They wore clothing made from the bark of trees, and cultivated little fields on the steep hillsides.

Another unknown tribe, found living on top of a grassy

plateau, cultivated such excellent fruit and vegetable allotments that they would have won praise from any British gardening expert.

The existence of these and other tribes had long been suspected, but no explorer had been able to reach them. Travel across the jungle-covered surface of New Guinea is not only difficult, but dangerous. There are no roads, only narrow winding trails hemmed in by trees and vines, where ambush by hostile natives is easy. In addition, the natural obstacles sometimes prove nearly insurmountable: crocodile-infested rivers and fever-haunted swamps, cliffs and gorges, and desolate places where food was unobtainable.

Another story which circulated among airmen, gold-prospectors, traders and police patrols concerned the existence of a "Lost Valley" in northern New Guinea. In a deep valley never reached by white men there was supposed to dwell a strange race of woolly-headed natives who were ruled by a woman chieftain. The coastal tribesmen spoke of the valley with awe, and declared that it meant death to try and reach the place. The valley was supposed to lie somewhere in the unexplored Loranje Mountains. Several expeditions tried to ascertain the truth of the story, but the difficult terrain which they had to traverse compelled them to turn back.

So matters stood until the last months of the Second World War, when the necessity of establishing an air route across Dutch New Guinea, from Hollandia to Merauke, finally led to the discovery of the hidden valley. The reconnaissance officers of the U.S.A.A.F. were given the task of surveying the route and establishing emergency landing-fields and radio bases. As much of the territory traversed by the air route was marked on the maps as "unexplored" the job was not an easy one.

The mountain country a hundred and fifty miles southwest of Hollandia proved the main obstacle, for although Mount Carstens, 16,400 feet, was believed to be the highest summit in New Guinea, the pilots now found themselves encountering peaks which topped 17,000 feet. More often than not the summits were enveloped in cloud, and it was only on rare occasions that the highest peaks were visible.

One day, while an aeroplane piloted by Pilot-Major M. Grimes was surveying part of the route, the clouds lifted for a short time and he saw a long, deep valley lying below. The outlines of numerous fields were clearly visible, with villages of round huts dotted here and there. Then the clouds shifted again and the "Lost Valley" was lost to sight. Curiously enough, Major Grimes had never heard the story of this legendary valley, but he recorded the discovery in his report, which in due course was carefully studied by the military authorities.

The air route became an established fact, and hundreds of aircraft flew backwards and forwards along it, but because of the clouds which almost perpetually shrouded the high peaks, few pilots ever sighted the secret valley. Gradually, however, various details were added to our knowledge of this strange survival from the distant past. It was proved that the valley was about five miles wide and about twenty miles long, and separated from the outside world by gigantic precipices and mountain peaks. The floor of the valley was criss-crossed by numerous canals, which argued a fairly advanced knowledge of agriculture.

A curious feature of the villages was the high look-out towers of bamboo poles, with platforms on top where sentries kept watch for parties of raiders. This indicated that life in the valley could not be as peaceful and undisturbed as one would imagine. Occasionally the pilot of one of the aeroplanes, anxious to obtain a closer view, would dive down below regulation altitude and fly over the watchtowers. Sometimes the sentries fled, but very often they remained at their posts and flung their spears at the approaching aircraft.

One day a parcel of trade goods, small mirrors, beads, strips of coloured cloths, and other things for which natives have developed a liking, was dropped by parachute. Later observers reported no sign of the package, which had apparently been opened and its contents distributed among the tribesmen.

On May 13, 1945, a transport aircraft carrying twenty-four American troops was forced off its course by a violent tropical storm and found itself hurtling down into the Lost Valley. A titanic wall of rock loomed up ahead, and though the pilot strove desperately to avoid a head-on crash, he was unsuccessful. All but three of the Americans on board were killed, and the blazing wreck of the plane plunged down to the valley floor. It was the first time white people had ever reached the hidden valley.

The three persons who survived were Lieutenant John McCollom, Sergeant Kenneth Decker, and Corporal Margaret Hastings of the W.A.A.C. In view of the curious happenings which followed it was fortunate for the two men that they had Corporal Hastings with them; but for the woman they might have been killed without mercy. For it was not long before the three made the astonishing discovery that the Lost Valley was ruled by a woman, an autocrat who maintained her own harem of a dozen or so men, and ruled the tribesmen with an iron hand. The truth of the old legend was rapidly being proved.

It was while the three were engaged in the unpleasant duty of burying their dead companions that the natives made their first appearance. Dark-hued men armed with long spears were seen approaching, led by a woman, whose costume consisted solely of a girdle made from pig's hair. The rest of her body was covered with red clay in startling designs. It was quite evident, by the deference with which she was regarded, that she was the ruler of these people.

To the surprise and dismay of Lieutenant McCollom, this dusky queen quickly made it clear that she regarded Corporal Margaret Hastings, and not himself, as the leader of the three. After pinching the corporal to make certain that she was real the native girl proved very friendly, and ordered her followers to bring food for the castaways to eat. In return Corporal Margaret had a package of trade goods opened, and offered the queen a number of presents. All this was very satisfactory; but the private thoughts of the two men at finding themselves relegated to a subordinate position in this feminist stronghold would make interesting reading.

Though they did not know it at the time, the three were destined to remain in the valley for six and a half weeks: it was not until forty-six days later that the military authorities at Hollandia were able to arrange for them to be rescued. So it is just as well that their first encounter with the natives was on a friendly basis. While they waited they were able to witness a way of life which had remained unchanged through centuries of isolation, an experience which is rare in the annals of modern exploration.

Army observers, surveying the valley from the air, had estimated that it could support a population of ten thousand. But the three castaways reported a much smaller number of natives. The people of the valley were, in fact, a dying race, having been decimated by tribal warfare through the centuries until comparatively few were left. Feuds and vendettas between neighbouring villages had caused big areas of the valley to go out of cultivation. What the civilized countries of the globe were trying to do with warships and bombing planes these primitive people had accomplished with spears, bows and arrows.

Lieutenant McCollom had managed to send out a radio signal to the base at Hollandia telling what had happened, and the military authorities immediately made an attempt at rescue. A transport plane loaded with supplies flew to the hidden valley, but, being unable to land, had to content itself with dropping food, radio, medical supplies and weapons by parachute. At first, when they had seen signal fires blazing in the darkness, the three survivors had feared that the natives might be cannibals, and were relieved when a dozen parachute troops under the command of Captain C. Walters were dropped into the valley by a transport plane.

However, the queen of this strange race remained friendly, and while the soldiers were exploring the valley trying to find a way out, Corporal Margaret and her companions were able to learn a great deal about them. A river which came foaming through the valley in furious rapids appeared to offer a way of escape, but though the natives negotiated the stream in bamboo rafts, it was soon perceived that no route to the outside world was possible. In any event, a journey over the trackless mountains to the coast would have taken months.

The possibility of building an air-strip upon which a plane could land and take off was next considered, but this also had to be abandoned. The project would have taken too long, there was insufficient labour and equipment, and even then the titanic peaks which enclosed the valley would have prevented an aircraft from gaining sufficient altitude to fly over them.

The problem of getting out of the valley daily grew more difficult of solution, and at the base camp at Hollandia discussions waxed fast and furious. For events had taken an unexpected turn; the "queen" of the valley had become so attached to Corporal Margaret that she invited her to join the tribe and become joint-ruler with her! Presumably the corporal could also have her own harem to choose from! But the ultimatum placed the white people in a dangerous position, for if the queen's request was refused, they might find themselves attacked by their hosts.

It was an officer at the base camp who made the suggestion which finally solved the problem. Why not have a pick-up glider towed into the valley and dropped where the castaways could board it? A tow-plane, moving at relatively low speed above the floor of the valley, could snatch the glider up again and tow it back over the mountains. And this is what was actually done. A glider, specially strengthened for the job, was launched into the valley, the castaways quickly scrambled on board, then the tow-plane manoeuvred into position, hooking the glider and whisking it into the air; a short time later they were across the mountains, and speeding swiftly back towards civilization.

And the Lost Valley with its dynasty of dusky queens is still there, if anybody cares to go and look for it.

Middle East

I

SKYSCRAPERS IN THE DESERT

*O*ne of the most interesting exploits of modern exploration was the discovery of a group of remarkable "skyscraper" cities in the little-known Hadramaut Valley of South Arabia. These skyscraper cities are oddly reminiscent of New York or Chicago, for their towering buildings, built of sun-dried brick, reach a height of ten and twelve storeys. But unlike their American counterparts these cities have walls and gates, for in Arabia the medieval and the modern exist side by side, and at any moment the townsmen may have to ward off attacks by Bedouin fighting-men from the desert.

Another curious thing about these cities is that though they are not linked by highway with the outside world, they possess motor-cars, telephones, radio, electric light, even private cinemas. Terim, Shibam and Seyun are the names of some of these cities, which, until the utilization of the aeroplane for map-making, had been seen by only a few Europeans. They are certainly one of the outstanding examples of contemporary Asiatic architecture.

What sort of land is it in which these curious cities exist? The country known as Hadramaut lies along the Arabian Sea, between Aden and Oman, and is bounded on the north by the Great Southern Desert. Makalla, three hundred miles east of Aden, is its chief port. It is ruled by a sultan under the protection of Great Britain, and the population is estimated at about a hundred and fifty thousand.

The country takes its name from the dry river valley known as the Wadi Hadramaut, the chief natural feature of the district. This great valley is over four hundred miles long, and though there is water in its upper reaches the lower reaches are always dry. The fertile districts produce dates, tobacco, wheat, millet and indigo; frankincense and myrrh are also produced, though the fabulous days of the incense trade are long since past. It is along the upper reaches of the valley that the group of skyscraper cities is found. How old they are no one can tell, for they appear to have existed for centuries without change and may have been there when the Romans first crossed the Channel to conquer Britain.

For two thousand years Arabia was a legendary land to the peoples of Europe, the exotic country whence came the frankincense which was burned on the altars of Rome, Thebes, Jerusalem, and a score of lesser cities. Frankincense is obtained from a tree of the genus *Boswellia* having a very short trunk and ash-coloured bark: incisions are made in the branches, and from these exudes a green transparent gum which hardens into the form of the sweet-smelling resin known as frankincense. Huge quantities were needed formerly for funerals and religious ceremonies, and as south-western Arabia was the principal source from which these supplies came, the trade became the country's chief source of wealth.

Southern Arabia was cut off from the rest of the world by the sea on the south and great deserts on the north. Across the deserts there developed an incense route which grew into one of the most rigidly-guarded trade roads in the world. Along it rose great cities which grew rich from the tolls collected from traders passing through their territories. Pliny (VII, 42) described the frankincense route and the great city of Sabota, with sixty temples inside its walls, and "a single gate left open for admission". The ruins of Sabota, known to-day as Shabwa, can still be seen in the desert country beyond the Wadi Hadramaut.

As the trade in frankincense declined another trade increased in importance, the spice trade. The peoples of Europe, lacking the benefits of refrigeration, required spices from the Orient to render their meat more palatable. So the cities in Hadramaut Valley, situated in a land possessing little natural wealth, continued to grow rich on the traffic passing between India and Egypt. For besides spices, other costly objects were now brought along the old incense roads; diamonds and sapphires from India, dates and slaves from the Persian Gulf, gold and ivory from East Africa.

Then came the change which brought to an end this age-old traffic, the discovery that the monsoon winds would enable ships to make sure and speedy journeys across the Arabian Sea to India, thus avoiding the long and toilsome journey across Arabia, with the necessity of having to pay toll to every petty chieftain in order to cross his territory. The old incense roads declined and became little-used, the cities which had grown up alongside them fell into decay. For centuries southern Arabia remained a blank area on the map to the outside world. But the long-forgotten cities survived, preserving through the centuries a strange and lovely architecture of a type hardly to be found anywhere else in the world.

The interior of Hadramaut was never easy of access, for though the coastline had been surveyed by various British naval expeditions during the late eighteenth and early nineteenth centuries, the twentieth century had almost dawned before Europeans first reached the upper valley and saw the many-storeyed cities, with their great castles and market-gardens. Southern Arabia had always been of special interest to the English, for the rich trade of the Persian Gulf region early attracted the attention of the East India Company, who established friendly relations with local rulers.

The inland part of Hadramaut remained unknown until 1843 when Adolf von Wrede, a Bavarian soldier who had lived for some time in Egypt, made the first journey into the interior. He crossed the country from the sea tto the Great Southern Desert, but the population was so fanasically hostile to Europeans that he was captured by the tribe men, and after being nearly killed for spying, was sent back to the coast. He did not reach the Wadi Hadramaut proper, which was not penetrated until fifty years later by Leo Hirsh, who was the first European to see the skyscraper cities of Shibam, Seyun and Terim.

In the same year a party led by James Theodore Bent also reached the upper valley and took the first photographs of the forbidden cities. "The buildings in the Hadramaut towns," Bent wrote, "were exceedingly high, reaching sometimes to eleven storeys. Built of sun-dried brick, decorated with chevrons, zigzag patterns, turrets, machicolations and buttresses, they had quite a medieval appearance. Flocks and herds were kept in the courtyards and stabled at night. The first floor was used for storage, the second by servants, the third by guests, and the others by the harem and family."

Bent's narrative of the journey tells how drainage was by open shafts into the yard below, and that there was a bathroom to each storey, equipped with a large jar of water and a receptacle for pouring it over the body. Windows were of various sizes. Those nearest the ground were only small holes for shooting through, upper ones were more spacious, with carved lattices, for members of the harem to look out from. No chimneys were visible, for these were cleverly disguised in the parapets or decorations of the roof. The bricks of which these great structures were built were made of mud mixed with straw-stubble. After being left for six days to dry, they were embedded in a mixture of mud and water which took the place of mortar.

The accounts of later travellers show that in essentials the towns of the Hadramaut Valley had changed but little: but an expedition in the spring of 1931, led by Dr. D. van der Meulen and Dr. H. von Wissman, a German geographer, found several surprising innovations. They found the wealthy inhabitants of the skyscraper cities driving about in motor-cars, talking by telephone to their neighbours, listening to their own cinema shows. The old cities had modern houses built in walled gardens in the suburbs. The cars had been brought from the coast in sections on the backs of camels.

It was want of space, as in New York, which had created the skyscraper cities of Hadramaut. The travellers considered Seyun the most beautiful city in the country, and they were impressed by the imposing buildings which the townsmen had created out of such simple materials as mud and a few crooked timbers. "Whether it be the poor man's hut, an imposing fortress, a beautiful villa, or a mosque with its graceful minarets, every edifice here is made of sun-baked mud." The hygenic arrangements, however, were less pleasing. "Gutters of hollowed-out palm-stalks jutted out from the kitchens, bathrooms and toilets, and the fluid waste poured down from the various levels into the streets below. Running through the middle of the streets are open masonry drains, clogged with garbage, on which chickens, cats and donkeys feed. We had to walk warily, with our eyes continually uplifted, ready to dodge any rain of filth from above."

More details of these cities and the way of life lived there were collected by Freya Stark, an explorer who has written in a gifted manner of a little-known part of Persia. Starting from Makalla in 1935 she crossed the stony plateau known as the Jol, which separates the upper Hadramaut valley from the sea, and visited a number of towns. Her ambition was to reach the ruined city of Shabwa, but she was prevented by illness from doing this. She brought back some excellent photographs of Shibam, Seyun and Terim, and these, together with aerial photographs taken by members of the R.A.F., constitute a striking pictorial record of this part of Arabia.

It was her belief that these many-storeyed Hadramaut houses had remained unchanged in type since prehistoric times, as the poet 'Alqama had described them when the Moslem missionaries first reached this country. (I quote the translation from Miss Freya Stark's book *The Southern Gates of Arabia*.)

> The proud Ghumdan and its dwellers. And this comfort for
> those who come after.
> It climbs the height of heaven, in twenty stories:
> The clouds its turban; girdle and cloak are marble;
> Its stones are fastened with dropping lead; jewels and marble
> lie between its towers.
> At every corner the head of a flying eagle; or of a bronze lion,
> roaring.

A water-clock on its summit; it drips to count the parts of day.
The birds halt upon it; and the waters flow in its channels
. . . and a look-out place is above
Of smooth marble, where the lords may stand; entrance is easy
to them.

At some time during the centuries these great palaces
began to be constructed, not of stone but of mud bricks. As
the wealth and prosperity of the valley declined their magnificence faded, but though they were no longer embellished
with marbles and precious metals they still remained imposing buildings. Freya Stark, watching the construction of
a new skyscraper, observed that only the lowest courses
were of stone; the rest of the tower was built of mud brick,
about eighteen inches square and three thick, set in liquid
mud. The walls thus produced were so massive that they
would stand for hundreds of years, and rain could scarcely
penetrate them. To counteract the crumbling tendency of
the mud the walls were built with a pronounced batter, and
the upper parts of the houses were decorated with alternate
bands of whitewash. In fact, the prosperity or poverty of a
family could be gauged by the amount of whitewash with
which they could afford to decorate their walls.

The interiors of such houses prove confusing to Europeans, for owing to the fact that for reasons of defence the
lower storeys are not provided with windows, they appear
as a labyrinth of dark, winding passages and rooms. The
upper storeys are divided into various apartments belonging
to different members of the family, each apartment being
provided with its own bathroom and sanitation. A niche
filled with clods of sun-dried earth takes the place of toilet
paper. Each storey had its *mussack*, or water-skin, which
was hung in a draught for coolness, and from which water
for drinking and cooking could be drawn.

Particularly noticeable is the wood-carving on doors,
beams, cupboards, and around the unglazed windows. A
great variety of patterns are used in the carving. Few windows are glazed, owing to the difficulty of transporting
glass overland from the coast. The windows are usually
protected by thick wooden shutters to keep out bullets,

for even now these houses are likely at any moment to become fortresses. Feuds between different families may lead to open warfare between neighbouring houses, and end in an exchange of rifle fire. The flat roofs at the top of the building are set apart for the ladies of the harem, and from this lofty vantage-point they can look down at the fighting taking place below.

The ceilings of the rooms are of palm-wood, supported on carved wooden pillars. The walls are covered with mud which is smoothed and whitened until it glistens as though it had been distempered. The builder's artistic sense, in simplicity of line and colour, is shown by their use of such features as two different kinds of windows, of plain bands of ornamentation, of machicolations for decorative purposes. There is little furniture in the rooms; the floors are covered with rugs, the walls decorated with brass trays and mirrors, with a few carved wooden chests for holding personal possessions. Such chests are also used to hold collections of ancient Arabic manuscripts which are the prized possessions of the more educated townsmen.

What of the people who live inside these skyscraper dwellings? Technical details of these remarkable buildings are not lacking; less is known of their inhabitants. That the people of Hadramaut are Arabs, whose ancestors were there long before the followers of Mohammed arrived to preach the new faith, is common knowledge, but they differ markedly from the better-known nomad Bedouin tribes of north Arabia. The big black tents of the nomad Arabs are absent; the big mud fortress with its walls and gates and towers is more in evidence. But until comparatively recently the details of life were much the same, with sheiks and emirs exercising patriarchal and despotic authority over the various districts, and the sultan as nominal ruler over all. Tribal warfare and blood feuds were part of the accepted order of things, and because of the insecurity of life and property, various fertile oases went out of cultivation because no man's life was safe.

Largely within the past decade or so this insecurity has given way to a more settled and secure mode of existence, with the Sultan and his governors wielding effective power over most of the countryside. This change-over to a strong government control is due to a large extent to the presence of the R.A.F. For nearly half a century much of Hadramaut had been linked with Great Britain by a series of treaties, but these had been of little effective use until the autumn of 1929 when a flight of the R.A.F. landed at Makalla from Aden, and proceeded to photograph the whole district. Numerous reconnaissance flights were carried out, and the positions of all places of importance accurately determined.

In 1934 a number of landing-fields were established, and the value of the aeroplane for policing hitherto inaccessible territories soon became evident. Local chieftains were not slow to realize the value of having a landing-ground near their homes, for aircraft were not only an effective means of ensuring peace among turbulent tribesmen, but by safe-guarding caravan routes they provided an increased source of revenue. The establishment of a native police force also helped to put an end to inter-tribal warfare and encouraged farmers to settle on the abandoned cultivated areas.

It was the absence of transport which had kept the country unspoiled, yet the skyscraper cities were as modern in some ways as any English or American town. How this curious state of affairs came about makes interesting reading. The desert conditions prevailing in a great portion of Hadramaut made it unable to support a large population, so many of the inhabitants emigrated abroad. The Hadrami native had always been possessed of an adventurous spirit, travelling to distant places as sailor or merchant, so many went to East Africa, others to India and the Dutch East Indies. From these places the emigrants regularly sent money enabling their families in Hadramaut to keep the homes going. For though the emigrants remained away from their homes for fifteen or twenty years, they always planned to return there.

Thus in Hadramaut one sees many fine palaces and other buildings, yet there is little natural wealth in the country to provide them; this anomaly is due to the money acquired in the commercial centres of India, Java and elsewhere. To-day most of the eighty thousand Arabs in the East Indies are from Hadramaut, while the Sultan spends most of his time in Hyderabad.

The Arabs, while abroad, also acquired a liking for such modern amenities as electric light, telephones, motor-cars and radio. When, having acquired sufficient wealth to enable them to retire, they returned to their homes in that distant and little-known valley, they brought these things back, with the result that superficially this almost inaccessible land appeared modern. There is also a tendency to replace their mud palaces by ones made of cement, though as a building material the latter is by no means the best. European styles of architecture are also making their appearance in the country, imported via India and the East Indies: the influence of Indian life and thought is very evident.

The resulting blend of the sophisticated and the primitive produces an incongruity which several writers have commented upon. For the Hadrami people, while abroad, appear also to have acquired a distrust of Europeans, and a determination to keep their valley as free as possible from such influences. It is a common fallacy to suppose that modern inventions inevitably aid in the opening-up of the world; on the contrary they can also be used to render a country more inaccessible should its inhabitants desire this. The history of such a country as Tibet illustrates how a native population can use such inventions as the telegraph, radio, and the motor-car to keep the hated European out of their country.

As a result of these conflicting attitudes there are developing in the Hadramaut two parties, one for and the other against European civilization, and who can say which will prevail?

VALLEY OF THE CRUSADERS

If asked to name the highest mountains in Europe, many persons would suggest Mont Blanc or the Matterhorn, without realizing perhaps that there is in Europe a range of mountains which possess no less than nine peaks higher than the highest Alpine summit. This range is the little-known Caucasus Mountains, lying between the Black Sea and the Caspian Sea, and separating Europe from Asia; its highest summit is Mount Elbruz, 18,526 feet high, or nearly three thousand feet higher than Mont Blanc.

This great mountain barrier is a region of contrast and contradiction, with scenery ranging from snowfields reminiscent of the Arctic to deep valleys filled with fields of tobacco, cotton and other tropical plants. An equal variation is shown in the various tribes and races which inhabit this region and who speak many different languages. Since the dawn of recorded history the Caucasus has been racially a sort of No-Man's-Land, a place of refuge "where fragments of forgotten peoples dwelt" and to which there drifted during the centuries odd tribes of Turks, Tartars, Persians and others. I remember even encountering a number of negroes, who looked very much like their counterparts one sees among the cotton fields of the southern United States, and was told that they were the descendants of a shipload of slaves which had been wrecked on the shores of the Black Sea nearly two and a half centuries ago.

The Caucasus have their full share of legends of curious peoples who live in the almost-inaccessible heart of the mountains, cut off from the outer world by high peaks and deep gorges. Mount Elbruz was reputed, by tradition, to be a resting-place of the Ark of Noah, after the Flood. Another and most persistent legend concerned the existence of a race descended from a party of Crusaders who lost their way while trying to reach the Holy Land in the twelfth century. They had retained the armour, shields and swords used by their Crusading ancestors, and employed these on raids among the neighbouring people of Daghestan.

That this was more than a legend was proved during the First World War, when Russian agents reached the remote Khevsoor Valley where these people dwelt. The various tribes inhabiting the Caucasus had long resisted the advance of the Russians, and though the region finally bcame incorporated in the Russian Empire, much of it remained unknown and unexplored. During the First World War the region was the scene of prolonged fighting between the Russians and the Turks, and a party of Khevsoors wearing armour and carrying shields and broadswords actually rode into Tiflis, the capital of Georgia, to offer their services in the fight against the infidels. Since then the Caucasus have become incorporated in a group of Socialist Soviet republics, including Armenia, Azerbaijan, Abkhazia, Daghestan, and others; roads have been built, schools and hospitals established, and other benefits of civilization imposed upon the not always grateful mountaineers.

I first heard of the Khevsoors while on a visit to Tiflis, now known as Thilisi, some years before the outbreak of the Second World War, and made an unsuccessful attempt to reach the remote valley in which they lived. One was able to go by car to a point about ninety miles north of Tiflis, but from there the route was along a rough trail accessible only to persons on foot or on horseback. It was a difficult and even dangerous journey, for the trail winds along the edge of steep cliffs and canyons. When the pass is blocked by ice and snow the valley is quite inaccessible.

Unfortunately, it was already late in the year when I made my attempt, and it was beginning to snow when we started to cross the ridge which separates the valley from the outside world. My guide warned me that it was foolhardy to continue, as even if we reached the nearest Khevsoor village in safety we might be unable to return, and would have to remain there until the following spring. For five months of the year the valley is completely isolated. So, reluctantly, I was compelled to forgo a visit to these strange people, and I turned back. But as I had managed to gather a certain amount of information about the Khevsoors and their history my journey was not entirely wasted.

Since then the Soviets have gradually extended their influence in the mountains, imposing a policy of collectivization upon the various tribes, and educating and developing them in accordance with the best Marxist principles; so it is quite possible that the Khevsoors, as an interesting and unique survival of the past, no longer exist.

Outwardly the Khevsoors, or Khesurs, differ but little from a score of other clans and tribes which dwell in the Caucasus. They are grouped in a number of villages, each living a communal life, and largely dependent on their herds of sheep, goats and cattle. Barley is their main crop. They are largely self-supporting, they produce most of their own food, build their own stone houses, make their own tools and clothing. In appearance they are tall and wiry, and wear the home-spun shirts, baggy trousers and black sheepskin hats common to the men of the mountains. It was the custom for each man to carry a rifle and have a couple cartridge belts criss-crossed across his chest.

What does distinguish the Khevsoors from their neighbours are the suits of ancient chain armour and swords inscribed with the letters "A.M.D." (which might mean *Ave Mater Dei*, i.e., Hail, Mother of God), a system of duelling governed by a rigid code of ethics, and their legendary descent from the Crusaders.

According to this legend a party of Crusaders from Lorraine, under the leadership of Godfrey of Buillon, while trying to reach the Holy Land, were shipwrecked on the shores of Turkey. Cut off from the main party of Crusaders by a horde of Saracens they had no choice but to retreat inland, and eventually reached the Caucasus. Unable to find the way back, they seized women from neighbouring villages, and settled down where they were. And there their descendants have remained. There seems little reason to doubt the truth of this legend, but should anyone do so,

Khurajbah—"one of the 'skyscraper' cities in the little-known Hadramaut valley of South Arabia."

Typical Hadramaut country

then they will have to explain the armour, the swords and the system of duelling.

I was told that the armour was genuine twelfth-century date and of French make. The chain armour was formed of thousands of hammered iron links, constituting a flexible garment which fitted the body like a shirt. A helmet made of the same material was drawn over the head, and long gauntlets for the arms and greaves to cover the legs completed the protection. Each outfit weighed about thirty pounds. The armour was worn only on ceremonial occasions, and when not in use hung on a nail in the living-room of the house.

Attempts had been made to manufacture suits of mail from copper wire stolen from the telegraph line running alongside the highway from Tiflis, but these had not proved very successful as they did not provide sufficient protection from sword thrusts. The original armour was now getting very rusty and dilapidated as the owners did not know how to preserve it properly. Their swords, incidentally, were about thirty inches long and were straight, two-edged weapons of typical Crusader type. The shields were small and circular, about eighteen inches in diameter, and made of leather embossed with a crude Crusader cross.

Duelling is also a legacy from the long-distant past, and is conducted according to centuries-old rules. As well as being the accepted way of settling disputes, it is also regarded as a sport, and part of the training which every boy and young man must undergo. Duelling is, in fact, almost the only sport or diversion open to the men of the valley, except getting drunk on barley brandy or raiding Daghestan villages and driving off their cattle (and nowadays the local soviet government discourages these activities and sends the raiders to jail). The Khevsoors fight for the sheer joy of it, and need little or no excuse to put on their armour and have a whack at each other with their long swords.

My guide over the mountains described to me how such a duel was conducted. Duels take place on an open space outside the village. Dressed in their armour the two combatants faced each other, shield held in one hand, broadsword in the other. At the sign to "Begin" they leap at each other, slashing and stabbing, parrying blows, whirling round and round like a couple of fighting-cocks. The sword blades clash against each other, slither across the armour, or rattle against the leather shields, which are used for parrying blows rather than taking their full force. As both fighters may have had a good swig of brandy before the duel commenced, many blows go wild, and although the noise and excitement are considerable, little actual damage is done.

These hand-to-hand combats differ in one respect from the jousts and tournaments of Crusading times, when women as well as men were spectators; here only men are allowed to watch, except on certain occasions. Yet curiously enough, one custom from the Middle Ages which has been retained is that of allowing a woman to stop a duel by dropping her handkerchief between the two fighters. As wounds or serious damage are rare, this seldom happens; for usually a few bruises are the only outcome. In more serious cases, when a man is badly wounded, his opponent has to pay compensation, usually a certain number of cows.

In common with other mountain tribes, the Khevsoors retain the bloody and destructive practice of the blood-feud. Should one villager be killed by another, whatever the reason, the dead man's heir is in honour bound to kill his father's slayer. And that man's son must in turn kill the man who killed his father. And so it goes on from one generation to another, until there is hardly a family in the mountains which is not involved. Neither logic nor common-sense is allowed to prevail, and the fact that the original killing may have been in self-defence is not allowed to interfere with the course of "justice".

This ancient code of honour has been the cause of more bloodshed than actual warfare. Whole families have been wiped out, fertile valleys have been rendered uninhabitable, because these vendettas spread like a form of blood-poisoning through the social structure. It often happens that a man is informed by the village elders that he must kill So-and-So because So-and-So's family have killed a relative of his. He may be a friend of So-and-So, or may not know him from

Adam, but kill him he must, knowing that he himself will be killed in turn by the dead man's avengers. And so the bloody cycle of killings continue, without any means of stopping it. Should any man be unwise enough to point out how foolhardy the practice is, point out its futility and waste of human life, he is ostracized by his fellow villagers. If he does not play the part of the avenger and satisfy the honour of his village, no man will work with him, no woman will look at or speak to him, his own family will not have anything to do with him. He must kill, and be killed in turn.

In other ways the Khevsoors resemble various primitive tribes of the Asiatic borderlands. Women occupy a very inferior position in the household. They eat after the men, not with them, and sleep in a separate room, on the floor, for only the men have beds. They marry young, usually at about the age of fifteen, and when pregnant have to lie in the goatsheds until the child is born, in order not to defile the house. The husband fires his rifle over the goatshed to drive away the evil spirits, but is not allowed to go inside it. Women have to work in the barley fields or tend the sheep and goats, and owing to the hardness of their lives they look old before they are thirty.

I wished that it had been possible to learn more about these strange primitive people, who seemed to have forgotten the knowledge which their ancestors had brought from far-off Lorraine. Although they used Christian symbols, and had a shrine in the village where occasional worship took place, they had only the vaguest ideas about Christianity. Most of the arts and crafts known to the Crusaders were forgotten and, until the arrival of the Russians, reading and writing were unknown. It is an instance of a civilized race relapsing into barbarism.

Often I wonder, when I read of the remarkable developments which are taking place within the Soviet Union, whether a visitor to Khevsoor Valley still gets the feeling of having stepped back into another age, the age of the Crusading knights, or whether the standardized Marxist culture has obliterated all traces of this, and whether the Khevsoor villagers nowadays know more about tractors and aircraft than Crusaders and duelling. For all I know to the contrary their battle-cry may be now the familiar "All power to the Soviets!"

Asia

I

THE DEAD CITIES OF CEYLON

*I*n the heart of the island of Ceylon, rising from the thick jungles, are architectural treasures echoing the splendours of centuries long past. Here are to be seen the ruins of Anuradhapura, once a huge and flourishing city having a population of between two and three millions. Now dreams to restore the ancient capital are coming true, for a modern city is being planned by the Sinhalese Government and has already been inaugurated. This new city is to cover an area of 3,000 acres, and it is an inspiring symbol of the energy and national pride to be found in the people of this important Dominion.

For many centuries the great ruins of Anuradhapura and other nearby cities lay forgotten, with the jungle ever encroaching on the decaying buildings. It was just over a century ago that a young English officer came upon them, but it was not until 1871 that any steps were taken to reclaim and preserve them. In recent years much work has been carried out under Government auspices to preserve the architectural wealth of ancient Lanka, as old Ceylon was called.

To-day Anuradhapura is easily reached from Kandy—a distance of ninety miles. The countryside through which you pass consists of plantation, forest, jungle and even desert. At the ancient capital there is good hotel accommodation, so that there is little or no hardship in visiting some of the most amazing ruins in the world.

The story of Anuradhapura dates back over two thousand years. Strangely enough, although the Sinhalese have little in the way of an ancient literature, yet in that wonderful book the *Mahawansa* there are chronicles surpassing any-

133

thing other nations can show. From about 500 B.C. up to the beginning of the British occupation in 1796 these historical records continue. And the fact that they are history and not sacred writings distinguishes them among a multitude of documents of equal antiquity.

The Sinhalese have a tradition of a great king who was the son of a lion, the word *Sinha* in their language and the origin of their own national name. This Sinha had a grandson, Wijaya, from whom the roll of the kings of Lanka begins. Wijaya came over from India on a raiding expedition and established himself in the island in 543 B.C. The original inhabitants of the island found by him on his advent are somewhat contemptuously spoken of in the records as *Yakkho*—demons. There is no record existing of these aboriginal inhabitants, although the few Veddas who live in the deepest jungles at the present day are a remnant of them.

Wijaya reigned for forty years and was succeeded by a nephew named Panduwassa. This ruler sought a wife from the land of his birth, and in due course his Indian consort arrived, accompanied by her six brothers who founded principalities and built cities, one of which, in honour of its founder, Prince Anuradha, was called Anuradhapura.

Anuradha and his sister, the Queen Bhoda Kachana, were the grandchildren of Amitodama, an uncle of the great Gautama Buddha. The city named in honour of the brother soon became the capital. It had been visited by the predecessors of Gautama, and in 307 B.C. it received his collar-bone, his begging-dish, and other sacred relics, among which was a branch of the Bo-tree under which the Gautama sat when he attained Buddhahood. This branch of the Bo-tree, according to the *Mahawansa*, was brought over from India by a sister of the royal missionary Mahindo, who successfully established Buddhism in Ceylon. The sacred Bo-tree still to be seen at Anuradhapura is claimed to be the growth of the identical branch brought over from India 2,200 years ago; and the antiquity of the tree, and its claim to being a genuine historical specimen of great age, can scarcely be questioned.

Tradition records that to the great city which grew up

here came merchants and travellers from distant countries to pay tribute and homage to the wealthy rulers of Lanka. Here, too, came Buddhist pilgrims from all parts of the eastern world. From Mongolia, from mysterious Nepal, from even more mysterious Tibet, all came seeking consolation, comfort and spiritual merit by contact with the relics of the most venerated religious figure in the Asiatic world.

It is clear then that Anuradhapura was a most important city. It was also a wealthy place because of its fame. Magnificent buildings were built: temples, palaces, mansions and various public works, the most interesting of which were the great reservoirs of water which served to supply the land by means of canals. These tanks, as they are called, in many cases exist to-day though dwindled in extent. The word "tank", however, is a misnomer; they resemble beautiful lakes, and form one of the most attractive features in a lovely country.

The reason for these reservoirs was the need to feed the huge population of the city. It is not easy to-day to realize that the countryside one passes through was once a rich agricultural area. The soil is fertile, and then the jungle was kept under control, thus enabling North Ceylon to become the chief rice-growing area of Asia.

At Anuradhapura there are many relics of its past glory, sufficient to show how great was the architectural skill of the ancient Sinhalese. Much also has been lost. By far the most striking survival is the group of 1,600 columns known as Lohopasada, or the Brazen Palace, built in the second century B.C., though subsequently often restored.

We have a most minute account of the building of this marvellous place in the *Mahawansa*. The king, contrary to the usual custom of his time, decided to pay his workmen, and before beginning deposited eight lacs of rupees and a thousand suits of clothing, and vessels filled with honey and sugar, at the four gates for their use. The palace rose to the height of nine storeys (afterwards reduced to seven), all covered with brazen tiles which shone like gold in the burning sun. It was surrounded by a polished wall broken by the four gates. Inside, the splendour was so great as to be almost unbelievable. Each storey contained one hundred apartments festooned with beads and flower ornaments consisting of gems set in gold. There was a gilt hall supported on golden columns in the centre, and besides the usual decorations this hall had festoons of pearls also. In the centre was an ivory throne with the sun on it in gold, the moon in silver, and the stars in pearls. As for the furnishing of this magnificent shell, it sounds like that of a modern house, for it was provided with chairs and couches and woollen carpets, all of the most costly materials of their kind, for it is particularly mentioned that even the ladle of the rice-boiler was of gold!

It is not exactly known with what intention this splendid building was founded; but it is supposed to have been the chief residence of the monks of the *Maha vihara*, the most important and oldest established community in Anuradhapura. This word *vihara* is applied to monasteries or temples in the *Mahawansa*; it refers always to some religious building and never to a secular one. A *vihara* seems to have been at first a hall or meeting-place of monks, and afterwards was used to signify a temple which may have included an inner shrine.

The gnarled grey monoliths are still standing in a perfect forest closely crowded together, and occupy the space of a fair-sized English cathedral. They are in forty parallel lines with forty pillars in each. The problem is how anyone could have found space to walk between them. This building underwent many vicissitudes, being thrown down by Maha Sena the "apostate" king in A.D. 286, and rebuilt by his son and successor. The last rebuilding was in the twelfth century.

I found it a curious sensation to stand alone in this stone forest, recalling the march of time and picturing the sombre flitting of the dark-skinned priests, and the many intrigues which were carried on within these precincts ages ago. But walls and pillars never talk, and all that one has is the imagination. Meanwhile the little striped, furry-tailed squirrels run up and down with a curious clockwork movement, and flitting lizards sun themselves and vanish.

Ruins at Polonnurawa, Ceylon

Rock Temple at Anuradhapura

Stone monoliths of the Brazen Temple, Anuradhapura

One of Ceylon's unique moonstones

Straight from the Bo-tree past the Brazen Palace runs the Sacred Road, which for hundreds of years was trodden by the feet of pilgrims. Overshadowed by spreading "rain-trees", bordered by green spaces, this ancient road was one of the great thoroughfares of Anuradhapura the Royal. Down it came in procession the halt and sick, eager to be cured, believing that the sight of the blessed Bo-tree would restore health.

On this road was the beggar making the most of his misery; the schemer; the braggart Pharisee; the humble-minded and devout; the woman aching for the joys and pains of motherhood; the mother yearning to see once again her long-missing son; the young boy on the threshold of life, awed by its mystery. Yes, along this now deserted track came those possessing the inexhaustible human virtue of faith. Also along this road, surrounded by his courtiers with flashing umbrellas and flags, came the despotic king, holding in his hands the lives of thousands of such as these; and maybe in his train followed the bloodthirsty prince, his near relative, scheming to dispossess him. They glide by, these shadows of the past, and then the vision falls away like a veil—the road is empty.

Another object that cannot fail to attract attention is the great dagoba Ruanweli. Of all the ideas that entered the mind of man this surely was the most extraordinary—to erect huge piles of stones in the shape of an inverted bowl, solid except for a tiny passage to a secret chamber which contained a relic.

To get an idea of this curious building, imagine the dome of St. Paul's Cathedral sliced off and set on the ground. The upper part of Ruanweli is to-day covered with green jungle scrub. Built over 2,000 years ago, this great mound is about 270 feet in height. Despite its still-existing religious importance, it seems to be no one's special business to see that tidiness is maintained and necessary repairs carried out.

Its construction must have been a colossal task, and, as in the case of the Brazen Palace, the labour employed was paid. At the consecration ceremony there was deposited in the secret chamber the largest and most important collection of relics ever enshrined together in one place—hence the peculiar sacredness of Ruanweli. At the ceremony bands played and the people came from all over the island in their thousands. When the sacred relics had been enshrined in a receptacle of great magnificence, the king also deposited all the royal ornaments he had on his person: then the priests closed the receptable with a stone, after which the people were allowed to put any relics they wished on the top of the shrine.

Ruanweli is not the largest of the Anuradhapura dagobas, however, coming third in size. It was originally surrounded by two large paved courts or platforms, the inner one raised above the outer. Round the outer side of the inner boundary wall there was originally a complete circle of elephants, made out of brickwork, each elephant being about nine feet high, and furnished, says the *Mahawansa*, with tusks of ivory. Most of these figures have fallen away beyond recognition; but in some the form of the animal is still discernible. The elephant was then, as it still is, an important factor in providing labour.

I have mentioned that the labour employed in this gigantic building was paid. However, it is recorded in the chronicles that as the people were too poor, after the Tamil wars, to make the enormous quantity of bricks required, heaven came to the pious monarch's aid, and, at King Sakra's orders, the god Wismakarma made them in a night at a spot sixteen miles distant, and then, taking the form of a lizard, pointed them out in the morning to a Vedda aboriginal, who was out there shooting with his dogs, and who hastened to inform the King of the miracle.

Abhayagiriya was the largest of the dagobas. When entire it was 405 feet high; its dome was hemispherical, and had a circumference of 1,130 feet. Its summit was therefore higher than St. Paul's, and 50 feet lower than St. Peter's. Although it is now in ruins, it has great charm, its unspoiled beauty making it the most attractive of the three great dagobas. Like Jetawanarama, the second largest dagoba, Abhayagiriya was built for commemorative purposes only: neither housed any relics.

The enormous shrine of Jetawanarama was built by a king about the close of the third century A.D. to mark his recantation of the errors of the Wytulian heresy, to which he had been a temporary convert. These heretical schisms played an important part in the history of Lanka, sometimes attaining considerable importance in the religious life of the people.

The height of this dagoba is 250 feet, and its diameter 360 feet; the cubic contents of the dome of brickwork and the platform on which it stands are estimated to exceed twenty millions of cubic feet. The materials used are sufficient to raise 8,000 houses, each with a twenty-foot frontage, and these would form thirty streets half a mile in length. They would construct a town about the size of Ipswich; they would line an ordinary railway tunnel twenty miles long, or form a wall one foot thick and ten feet high, reaching from London to Edinburgh. The work involved in its construction can thus be imagined, and its present-day cost would run into millions of pounds. But only the "glory of outline" is left to the Jetawanarama; its four chapels have crumbled away almost beyond recognition, enormous trees have eaten into the brickwork to the very summit and troops of the large grey wanderoo monkey are the only devotees who frequent the holy place.

To the west of Ruanweli is a most beautiful *vihara*, raised, as all were, on a platform, and approached by a moonstone and carved steps.

The moonstones of Ceylon are unique; in no other country are they found in this shape and style. How they originated is not known, but they must have been native to the island, for though many details of architecture were borrowed from India and influenced by Indian thought, the only representative of these stones in India is a poor thing without the peculiar animal symbols which are a feature of the Sinhalese type. It is unfortunate that these stones are known by the same name as the milky-blue jewel, also found in Ceylon and nowhere else, because much confusion has resulted, though the two bear no relation whatever to each other.

The architectural moonstones are semi-circular slabs of

stone, set at the foot of a flight of entrance steps, and wonderfully carved. To the fact that most of those who passed over them went barefoot we probably owe the fact of their remarkable preservation. The stone is divided into concentric rings, first and outermost a narrow, conventional design, then a wider band in which a procession of animals—elephant, horse, lion, and bullock—follow one another round; there are two complete sets of these animals, and the elephant being thrice repeated, beginning and ending the procession, makes nine figures in all. The elephants are excellently executed, full of fire and life, and differing from each other in detail. The bullocks are fair, but the horses are poor and the lions almost grotesque. The artist must have seen horses; lions he can never have seen, but it is odd that the lion should figure so prominently in Sinhalese tradition and carving when the living animal is in no way associated with the country and, as far as is known, never has been.

One of the great interests in these ruined cities of Ceylon lies in the fact that, thanks to the records in the *Mahawansa*, we have the truthful background behind many of the details. Because of this a visitor can profitably spend several days in exploration. As an example, consider the Miriswetiya dagoba. This was erected about the middle of the second century B.C. by King Dutugemenu. The reason for its erection gives a curious insight into the character of the pious ruler. He remembered one day that he had on a certain occasion partaken of a common accompaniment of curry known as "sambal" (wetiya), without offering a share to a priest. Remorsefully anxious to expiate the omission, he was prompted by a miracle to build a great shrine in honour of Buddha, and to call it Miriswetiya, after the dish which had necessitated the atonement.

There is so much to see at Anuradhapura, for at its prime it was a city as large as London in area. The distance between opposite gates, north and south, was sixteen miles, and they were linked by one straight street. In this one street there were eleven thousand houses, many of them being two storeys in height. The smaller streets were innumerable.

An excellent account of what the capital must have been

like in its heyday is given by Major Thomas Skinner in *Fifty Years in Ceylon,* for he visited the place on a road-making expedition in 1832.

"The line of the streets," he writes, "can still be traced. In them the bright-robed people, with whom were mingled thousands of yellow-robed monks, passed to and fro, while lordly elephants strolled along having passage made for them. Beyond the walls, from a distance, could be seen the golden roofs flashing in the sun against the thrilling blue of the sky. Inside, if it were a festival day, maybe the huge dome of Ruanweli would be one mass of flowers[1]—lotus, orchid, and jasmine—scenting all the air with an almost overpowering odour. There were great parks containing pavilions; peacocks strolled on the close-clipped grass between the flower-beds, and the vast stretches of mirror-like water were freely used for bathing. Around the Bo-tree rose a temple of several storeys, and there, as to-day, were always worshippers, silent, dark-faced, offering flowers and bowing themselves in reverence. Many of the lowest caste hastened along, watering the streets from skins to lay the dust. The grand buildings set among the trees gleamed like marble and were adorned with free bold carving and bands of gold and silver, and inside there were many pillared richly decorated halls, containing possibly thrones of gold and ivory, holding in corners great golden images of Buddha looking out from inscrutable jewelled eyes. And in various parts of this great city; hospitals where complaints are tended and healed; and on the outskirts great cemeteries for the burial of the dead."

Another account states:

"Anuradhapura was not one city but two, one within the other, and the royal residences and chief monastic edifices and dagobas were enclosed within walls of great strength, and shut in by massive gates, flanked by watch towers and guard houses. Beyond these limits was the outer city set apart for the lower orders, wherein the business life of the

---

[1] Of King Bhatikabhaya (19 B.C.) it is recorded that "he festooned Ruanweli, from the pedestal ledge to the pinnacle, with fragrant garlands four inches thick, and having stuck flowers in between, he made the whole one immense bouquet."

city was transacted. It consisted mainly of one long, wide
street, composed of shops for the sale of every description
of goods, and these were divided—as usual in Eastern cities
—into quarters for the various callings of provision-dealers,
drapers, goldsmiths, artisans, and even to the retailers of
children's toys, some of which have been found buried beneath the ruins of buildings. On the outskirts of the lesser
city were extensive tracts set apart for the growth of innumerable flowers, solely for the decoration of temples and
dagobas and for the ornamentation of the streets on great
Buddhist festal days."

From Anuradhapura to Polonnaruwa, to the south-east,
is a distance of some seventy miles. It was a royal city, for
although Anuradhapura held that position for some 1,400
years, the incursions of the Tamil invaders made it necessary
for the Sinhalese kings to move the seat of government to
a more protected position. The first capital lies on a flat
plain without any natural defences.

Polonnaruwa remained the capital until the end of the
thirteenth century. It has not the same area of ruins as the
original capital, but in many ways it is the more amazing
place. There is more of it left. Among the monuments are
one or two unique in themselves, and unlike anything
dreamed of elsewhere: such are Dalada Maligawa, the Wata-
dage, Floral Altar, and Lotus Bath, which are worth travelling thousands of miles to visit.

The Dalada Maligawa is the gem of Polonnaruwa. This
temple was built to receive the Tooth of Buddha (now kept
in Kandy), and it is still in a wonderful state of preservation:
the clear-cut figures and mouldings on the granite have
suffered little from time; and though most of the roof has
fallen in, the walls have been very little displaced. The
building, which is Hindu in design, consists of an outer
quadrangle and an inner and innermost shrine. It was in
this innermost shrine that the Tooth was probably kept.

The Wata-dage ("Circular Relic-house") is a building
formed by successive terraces or platforms, circular, one
rising above the other. It has four entrances at the cardinal
points, with guard-stones, moonstones, makara-scroll and

decorated risers of the stairs, but all differing from one another in detail. Of the beauty of some of this work it is impossible to speak too highly. The entrance to the east is perhaps the finest: here there is every kind of carving and stone lattice-work.

Another lovely gem in this architectural paradise is the Floral Altar or "Hall of the Flower-Trail". A space of some 34 feet by 28 feet is enclosed, and within it is a stone platform from which rise most curiously designed pillars. In the centre of the platform is a small dagoba. It is difficult to give an idea of the daintiness and originality which mark this architectural gem. The idea of the lotus flower runs all through it. The cone-shaped heads of the posts are the exact shape of those unopened buds. The head of each pillar standing on the inner platform originally showed carving representing an opening lotus. Some of these still remain. We may trace the lotus everywhere on this monument, in copings, on the heart of moonstones, on pillars and panels. Considerable work has of recent years been carried out in the restoration of this flower-shrine, and in one's memory of the Polonnaruwa monuments it is the one which is most vivid.

It is impossible here to mention even the many wonderful things still to be seen in Polonnaruwa and the other dead cities of Ceylon; but I would wish to say a few words about the Lotus Bath and the Royal Palace.

The Lotus Bath lies hidden away in the jungle: a wonder in stone, a flower petrified and preserved for immortality. The artistic conception of this beautiful bath is superb. Imagine a gigantic lotus-flower of granite, 25 feet in diameter, and dropping to a depth of five feet in diminishing rings, each forming a step, until it reaches the heart—the bath proper—five feet four inches across. This bath was probably used by the monks; it is of comparatively recent discovery, for it lies some miles outside the city.

Another striking feature of Polonnaruwa is the ruin of the former Royal Palace, with its traces of walls, many feet thick, still in position. From the chronicles we learn that Sinhalese ideas on the subject of housing royalty in the twelfth century in Ceylon were very much in advance of those in England at the same period.

A long time may be spent in tracing out the rooms of this palace. The spaciousness of the central rooms, probably occupied by the kings and queens, is remarkable. And the indications of privies, water-supply, and other conveniences indicate a very advanced civilization.

We are told that this palace had seven storeys and one thousand chambers supported by many hundreds of beautiful pillars. The building was surmounted by pinnacles, and its gates and doors were made of gold. In the king's bedroom there was always a perfume of flowers, and His Majesty "went to bed by the light of golden lamps from which were suspended strings of pearls."

Near the Royal Palace is the *Galpota* or Stone Book. It is so called from its resemblance to a volume of palmyra leaves. It is nearly thirty feet high, two and a half feet thick, and five feet broad. Inscribed on it is a long account of the virtues and great deeds of King Nissanka, and it concludes with the statement that this huge monolith had been brought from a mountain over 80 miles distant.

When one stands on the site of dead cities, the thought always comes to the mind as to why they died. Invariably their wealth and prosperity is coveted by others; in the case of Lanka, by the Tamil people who lived across the narrow straits that separate Ceylon from India.

There were constant invasions by these Tamils, but they never resulted in total conquest until, in the reign of King Mahinda V (A.D. 1001), disaster overwhelmed the Sinhalese. The kings had been in the habit of maintaining armies of Malabars as mercenaries: but this king, being a mild man, did not enforce the collection of revenue, and had no money to pay them, so they revolted. Thus the invaders had everything their own way; and, hearing how it was, more enemies came over from India and took all the spoil from the great cities and "like the demons who suck up blood, they took to themselves all the substance that was therein," and they carried the king away captive.

Hordes of new settlers now poured in, and the character

Four-faced towers, Bayon Temple, Cambodia

The Temple of Angkor Wat—still a place of pilgrimage

Terrace of Elephants, Angkor Wat

of the population changed. Despite a certain recovery by later Sinhalese monarchs, the rot of decay had set in. Prosperity waned. The ancient arts were forgotten, the agricultural pursuits neglected. Gradually the jungle took control, and fast-growing creepers and plants covered the masonry of the once-glorious buildings. The roots of great trees did the most damage for they attacked the foundations of the monuments, palaces, temples and houses.

This, then, was the end—the end of a marvellous civilization. The survivors abandoned their cities, and the jungle crept in—the greatest conqueror of all—and blotted everything out. Hundreds of years later in the seventeenth century the first Europeans—the Dutch—came and began the work of reclamation.

2

THE GLORY OF THE KHMERS

$\mathcal{I}$t is not easy nowadays for the traveller to visit Angkor; and this is a tragedy. For in this remote part of Cambodia there are the remains of a great city which are unexcelled both in conception and beauty. In all my wanderings I have never seen such magnificence. Buried deep in the dense jungle is the work of supreme architectural inspiration, and it is easy to understand the belief of the Cambodians that such buildings as the Angkor Wat and the Bayon were not built by man but by the gods themselves. Here, indeed, was the crowning glory of the Khmer civilization.

I arrived at Angkor just as the sun was setting. The great temple on my right was swathed in purple mist and shadow. Never had my imagination visualized such a spectacle. Its unexpected size, its glorious beauty, struck me like a flash. All the sweat and toil of my journey—for, in a tropical heat, I had laboriously cycled all the way from Saigon, some 400 miles—was repaid me in a moment. It brought a surge of inspiration to the soul.

There is a Cambodian legend which claims that there came a king from the west who married a cobra's daughter; and their children were the gods of ancient Cambodia. This is a pleasant fary-tale of the origin of the Khmers. Despite its improbability, it is probably just as correct as most of the other suggestions and claims made for the origin of this civilization. That is one of the pleasures of Angkor—that no one knows how things really did happen. All the experts have their own theories, most of them being of an opposite nature.

Until the last thirty years or so Angkor was inaccessible by road: the French have now opened it up. Previously the journey was made by boat—if the river allowed—to the

Lake Tonle-Sap, and then by ox-wagon to Siemreap. It was a trip for enthusiasts. To-day there is even a *de luxe* hotel at Siemreap, although tourists are few and far between.

Angkor remains a lost civilization. Through the centuries it has been a mystery—the "lost city of the East". Here was the capital of the Kingdom of Foonan, which once covered the area of present-day Malaya, Siam, and French Indo-China.

The first historical record is of an exchange of ambassadors between the Khmers and the Court of China in A.D. 243. A Chinese writer tells us that the Khmers paid their tribute to powerful China "in gold, silver, pearls, and perfumes". For five centuries Khmer ambassadors went to China bearing tribute. Then in the fifth century an important event occurred when a Brahman, who was possessed of supernatural powers, brought Indian influence into the country. This importation was to have a profound effect on the Khmers and to bring about the birth of that civilization which was to reach its peak some centuries later.

Angkor itself was begun about A.D. 877 by the king Yasovarman, but its final construction was delayed until about the year 944. For another two hundred years the kings continued to beautify it, and its greatest height was reached in the tenth and eleventh centuries, the jewel of Angkor architecture being the Angkor Wat, which was built about A.D. 1140.

Towards the end of the fourteenth century decay had set in. There had been constant wars between various claimants to the throne, and this resulted in considerable damage. But possibly what caused the real downfall and almost complete disappearance of the civilization was an invasion from Siam. In 1385 the Siamese captured Angkor and sacked it. They took the able-bodied people as slaves and killed off the others who were useless to them. Only five thousand managed to escape this terrible disaster. For some years the city carried on, but the Siamese returned in 1417 and besieged the Khmers. After a seven months' siege the inhabitants capitulated after their own ministers had gone over to the enemy. Most of the population departed with their conquerors. This is the last record of Angkor as an occupied city. During the sixteenth century Portuguese travellers referred to Yasovarman's work as an ancient city lost in the forest. But it was not until 1860 that a French traveller gave an accurate account of its re-discovery. At this time the lands of Angkor belonged to Siam, which had again seized them a hundred years previously, but the Franco-Siamese treaty of 1907 gave back to Cambodia its ancient capital, and it is only since 1908 that efforts have been made to clear out the heavy vegetation and disclose to the world one of its greatest wonders. Unfortunately lack of funds prevent operations on a fitting and necessary scale; so much of the city remains hidden.

It seems strange that this great civilization should have existed and disappeared with scarcely any record of it remaining. The only one is that given by a Chinese traveller Tcheou-ta-Kouan, who visited Angkor towards the close of the thirteenth century. He tells of a city wall with a circumference of about ten miles. This wall had two entrances on the east side and one entrance on each of the other sides. The centre city was surrounded by a wide moat crossed by causeways. On either side of the bridges leading up to the gates were fifty-four stone demons "like stone generals, gigantic and terrible". There were parapets on these bridges and they were sculptured in the shape of nine-headed serpents. The fifty-four demons held the serpent in their hands, and "looked as though they were preventing the serpent from escaping". On the city gates were five stone heads of Buddha, the central one being adorned with gold; and two sides of the gates were carved with elephants' heads. The wall was entirely built of superimposed blocks of stone . . . it was a regular square, and at the angles were stone towers.

Criminals whose toes had been cut off were not allowed to enter the gates. In the centre of the city was a golden tower, the Bayon, which was flanked by more than twenty stone towers, and hundreds of stone cellars. On the east side lay a golden bridge with two golden lions standing on either side. Eight golden Buddhas occupied stone chambers.

Tcheou records that half a mile to the north lay the king's

dwelling. He had his rooms set apart in a golden tower. The tiles of his tower were of lead, but all other buildings had yellow earthenware. The council hall had golden window-frames, below which were sculptured elephants. It was forbidden to enter the palace. The king used to sleep in the top of the golden tower. The natives believed there was a spirit there in the shape of a nine-headed serpent, master of the whole kingdom and the earth.

It appears every night in the form of a woman with whom the king must sleep. Even the king's principal women dare not enter. He leaves at the second watch and the king can then sleep with his wives and concubines. If one night the serpent spirit does not appear, the moment of the king's death has arrived. If the king fails to be there on a single night some misfortune takes place.

The dwellings of the princes and grandees were different in size and form from those of the common people. All out-houses were thatched: only family shrines and private dwelling-rooms were allowed to be covered with tiles. The official rank of each person determined the size and type of his house.

Everybody, from the king down, both men and women, wore a loose flowing garment, known as a sarong, which left the shoulders bare. But when they went out they added a voluminous outer garment. There were many qualities of cloth, and naturally the best were worn by the king, for whom the finest wool and silk were reserved. A great quantity of cloth was imported from other countries, although there was a certain amount of commoner cloth woven locally.

Only the king may wear a densely flowered material. He usually wears a golden diadem, but when he is without it he rolls some garlands of odoriferous flowers round his chignon. His necklace is made up of nearly three pounds' weight of large pearls. On his wrists, ankles, and fingers he wears bracelets and rings of gold set in "cats' " eyes. He goes barefoot and the soles of his feet and the palms of his hands are tinted with a red pigment. When he goes out he holds a golden sword in his hand (the sacred sword). Among the people only the women may tint the soles of their feet and the palms of their hands. High officials wear sparsely flowered cloth. The palace people may wear cloth decorated with a double row of flowers, but among the common people only the women are allowed to wear flowered cloth.

In the Khmer kingdom there were counsellors, generals, astronomers, and many officials. Princes were usually chosen to fill the high positions, but in certain cases those who offered their daughters as royal concubines were chosen.

In his account the Chinese traveller keeps on remarking on the great display of wealth which he saw on every side. The highest dignitaries were those who used a gold-shafted palankeen and had four gold-shafted parasols held over them. There were a great number of monks of various kinds. The Buddhist monks shaved their heads, wore yellow robes, and left their shoulders bare, just as they do to-day. The temples contained only one image resembling the Buddha Sakyamuni. The statue was dressed in red and was made of clay. On every side outside the temples were figures of Buddhas, but they were cast in bronze. "All monks eat fish and meat, but drink no wine. One meal a day is prepared in the kitchen of the host as there are no kitchens in the monasteries. The monks recite numerous texts which are written on bound palm leaves." There were not any Buddhists nuns. The king was wont to consult the monks on affairs of state, and religion played a great part in the life of the people.

Then there were the Brahmans: for one of the features of the Khmer civilization was its great religious toleration. The Brahman monks dressed like the ordinary people except for a piece of red material which they wore on their heads. Their temples were smaller than those of the Buddhists, but that was because Hinduism was not so flourishing as Buddhism. The Brahmans worshipped only a block of stone resembling the altar stone of the sun god. The Brahman monks did not eat in public nor did they eat the same food as other men, and they drank no wine. There were Brahman nuns.

The king had five wives. One was for his central apartment and one for each of the cardinal points. In addition there were from three to five thousand concubines. These latter were graded and divided into classes, but they were rarely allowed to go outside the palace. "As for me," wrote Tcheou, "each time I entered the palace I saw the King go out with the first Queen and sit at the golden window of his private apartment." The big palace required the services of two thousand women servants, but they were married.

When the king went out there were cavalry at the head of his escorts, then came standards, pennants, and music. Then followed palace girls to the number of three to five hundred who wore flowered robes and had flowers in their hair. They held large candles and marched in a body: even in daylight they carried lighted candles. Next came the palankeen with servants carrying gold and silver utensils, and a whole series of valuable ornaments. "All of an unusual type and of which the use is unknown to me."

Then came a troop of amazons, armed with lance and shield, who formed the king's bodyguard. They were followed by great cars and horse-chariots all adorned with gold. The king's ministers and the princes were mounted on elephants, and they had red parasols. Then there came the king's wives and concubines seated on palankeens, in carriages, and on elephants. They, too, carried parasols adorned with gold.

Last came the king, standing erect on an elephant and bearing aloft the precious sacred sword. The tusks of his elephant were bound with gold. The king was followed by twenty more elephants, their riders all having gold-shafted parasols. Such a procession must have been a most imposing sight.

When the king went out to visit, a little golden pagoda was held in front of him; and in front of this again was a golden Buddha. Those who saw the king had to prostrate themselves and touch the ground with their foreheads. If they did not do so they were fined. The king gave audiences twice daily in connexion with affairs of government. No definite list was prepared. Functionaries and people sat on the ground awaiting his appearance. Tcheou describes the interesting ceremonial connected with the appearance of the king.

After some time one hears a distant music: outside they blow trumpets in welcome. Two palace girls lift a curtain with their little fingers and the king appears, holding a sword in his hands. At that moment the ministers and people join hands and strike the ground with their foreheads. They may not raise their heads till the trumpets cease to sound. According to the king's pleasure and approval they approach and sit down before him on a lion's skin, which is regarded as a royal object. When the business is completed the king leaves; the two palace girls let the curtain fall, and everybody rises.

* * *

Reading this account of the past life of the Khmers, I found it easy to re-create those glorious scenes as I sat among the ruins of Angkor. In this apparently dead city I felt keenly the life of a past age. Out of the mysterious past I saw how their life and arts had grown to a climax of supreme glory, only to sink back into mystery once more. I spent some days exploring the district in order to get the right background, and also to make contact with the right person to help me. It was clear that there must have been enormous wealth in this country, and it was also obvious that precautions would have been taken by the wealthy people to prevent it falling into the hands of invaders.

Within the city itself, under the old Empire, there sprang up twenty temples, for which a mountain of sandstone was required. These were fashioned by sculptors of unrivalled skill. From Angkor numerous roads branched out into the surrounding country which embraced over eight hundred temples and shrines built by the kings. Where to-day there is impenetrable jungle, with here and there a few natives eking out a bare existence, there flourished in those days a thickly populated civilization supported by large areas of cultivated land.

What industry there must have been! On every side there would be stone-cutters at work engraving figures and inscriptions. Vast reservoirs were erected and a number of massive bridges were built. During all the period of its existence Angkor had to defend itself constantly against foreign foes, for to it flowed endless wealth—gold and silver and brass with which to crowd the temples and shrines with images and statues.

Angkor, which simply means "the capital", was the creation of the Khmer kings. Before it was built these monarchs travelled about building new capitals all over the country. It is not known why these wanderings were necessary, and very little is left of the cities they built. The jungle has grown around and over them. Angkor lies on a flat plain which to-day is almost entirely covered with jungle and dense forest, but which in the time of the Khmer occupation was cultivated and grew rice. This forest, which now encroaches on all sides, is therefore comparatively recent. The main part of the city, known as the Angkor-Thom, was the portion visited by Tcheou.

In the construction of these buildings both brick and sandstone were employed. The sandstone came from quarries about twenty-five miles away. No mortar was used, but the bricks and stone blocks were rubbed together to obtain perfect adherence. Strangely there was no knowledge of bonding in building. Wood was also freely used, but this has now largely vanished. The interiors of the buildings were richly decorated with gilt and paint. The Khmers were not clever builders, but their system enabled them evidently to build with great speed.

The main city within the walls was largely taken up with temples, monasteries, palaces, and the houses of the rich; the poorer part of the population made their homes outside the walls. Of all the temples which exist to-day in this land, the most important and beautiful are the Bayon and the Angkor Wat. Yet it is possible that hidden in the forest lie more temples of equal beauty.

The Bayon was the great central temple of the Khmer Empire. To the north of it, as described by Tcheou, lies the Royal Palace, and to-day the visitor can still see its wonderful terrace, with its façade of magnificently sculptured elephants of almost life size.

I made my first approach to the Bayon in the early morning when the dazzling rays of the sun lit it up. As I drew near I saw I was being peered on by massive human faces in stone which flanked all its towers like an assembly of giants. On all sides and on different planes there surged these architectural glories. Everywhere I found decoration and design; but between all these pyramids, towers, shrines, and terraces there is perfect balance and composition. It appears to be one of the perfect examples of human genius, and I was amazed at the mass of detail which does not detract from the splendour of the whole conception. There is vigour and dignity; there is breadth and variety and subtlety of ideas; and there is soul which makes everything fit into one illimitable plan.

This Bayon was the hub of the Khmer universe. It rises in three storeys on which are placed fifty towers and one hundred and seventy-two human faces. One of its charms lies in its sculptured terraces with bas-reliefs, showing scenes of most varied interest. There are dances, festivals, combats, and scenes representing the ordinary everyday incidents of life. Birds and animals people the scenes, and many of them are of an amusing character. The Khmers clearly had a well-developed sense of humour, for even priests were caricatured in the carved pictures.

From the third storey of this building I saw below me the domes and galleries of the second storey, and beyond them on every side was the vast forest which surrounded this island of stone. All around me were human faces, looking full-face, three-quarter face or profile. Some seemed to be smiling, and others looked solemn, but all had a sphinx-like mien which enforced on me a contemplation of the super-human. Time, indeed, was lost count of as I sat there buried in contemplation. I felt as though I were being carried away on powerful wings to the eternal. For in the complete silence which embraced this temple, I found that appeal to my imagination which is always more powerful than the spectacles afforded by nature. The latter awake no memories, and it is by memory that the mind is invigorated and refreshed.

I cannot describe here many of the other very beautiful temples and shrines which exist in this part of Cambodia. Some of them I found with difficulty for the jungle has grown right into them. I saw some of the difficulties which would face me once I started out myself to find my distant temple. Monkeys and gibbons and gaily coloured birds haunt the homes of the monasteries which once held thousands of monks, who lived and laughed and worked so many hundreds of years ago.

But I cannot omit a description of the greatest glory of all—the Angkor Wat—the temple which lies about a mile outside the city walls, and was within view right in front of the bungalow in which I was staying.

In the course of our short life it is hard to believe that one will ever see any other building which can excel in beauty that glorious temple. The conception is superb. With the afternoon sun shining on it there emerged a constant change of lights and shades, but the greatest glory was at sunset.

The approach is over a wide moat, a quarter of a mile wide. Having crossed this, I found myself at a gateway through which, framed against the horizon five hundred yards off, stood the main body of the temple. I found it difficult as I entered this temple to know what most to admire. On every side were sculptures and bas-reliefs. Every wall was covered with the most exquisite and delicate carvings. A whole panorama, changing and varying constantly, unfolded itself before me.

At the top lies the central shrine. Before I reached it by steep steps I wandered through courts and passages into which the setting sun filtered. On all sides were Buddhas, many of them broken and fallen down. All through the centuries this temple has been in active use and it is still a place of pilgrimage. Monasteries for the Buddhist monks lie just outside the entrance; as I wandered along passages I came upon yellow-clad priests praying to Buddha, and lighting joss sticks here and there. This sign of activity encouraged me to think that hidden away in the jungle would be another temple which had been tended and guarded through the centuries since the mysterious disappearance of the bigger civilization.

The temple is swept clean by the devotion of the local peasantry, which is fortunate for the visitor, as under all the roofs hang countless bats. As I walked about they were pouring out in huge clouds on their way to seek their food, only to return to their dark homes at early dawn.

The topmost shrine itself—the heart of the temple—is a dark cell only a few yards square, filled with the swish of frightened bats when I made my appearance. An overturned pedestal was barely visible in the darkness, covered with bats' excreta. That was all!

Misery, and a shrine bereft of its gods. Six centuries of architecture, many millions of men, vast quantities of stone dragged over plain and swamp, smoothed and carved, the whole genius of a race—all this for what? To bear in later days a shrine empty, obscure, and steeped in filth. The glory that was Foonan!

But if the gods have vanished, yet the grandeur attained by man remains. To sit under the archway and watch Angkor Wat reflecting the sun's last rays, varying from cold purple at its base to the rich deep red round its summit, was for me to feel that it was one of the supreme moments of my life.

Even the most unimaginative could scarcely fail to have visions in such a place. How many men expressed their feelings through these stones? How many kings must have felt that here they were building for eternity? I could almost visualize in the half-light the temples and courts filled with priests carrying on their devotions, discussions, and intrigues. Ancient monarchs holding audience with dance, play, and music appeared before me—and gods and symbols and myths.

The old kings practised tolerance and were liberal and humane. In the twelfth century it is recorded that Jayavarman VII founded one hundred and forty-two hospitals spread over his empire. That humane king "suffered more from the sickness of his subjects than from his own maladies and sorrows. For it is the sorrows of his people which caused the king's sufferings". Another king pitied the position of his people, "the common folk without any exception, the young, the aged, those who suffer, the unhappy, and those abandoned, are to be looked after carefully, fed, medically treated, and given all that is necessary".

There are records to show that justice was most impartially dispensed, and that exploitation of the poor by the rich was forbidden. Hunger and cold, two of the chief troubles of Western civilization, did not exist.

To-day the visitor sees the descendants of the ancient Khmers weaving baskets, ploughing, fishing, and playing the flute. Stones have been levelled: but one thinks of the lovely and good things gleaned from the past centuries.

3

DWELLERS IN PARADISE

There are many lovely places in this world of ours, but it would be hard to find any country more beautiful than Sikkim. This little-known semi-independent state which now comes undes the protection of India is wedged in between Tibet, Nepal, Bhutan and Northern Bengal. Here, surrounded by lofty mountains on three sides, live the Lepchas, who form about one quarter of the total population.

These Lepchas are descended from the original inhabitants of the state, but they are steadily decreasing in numbers. There are several reasons for this, but undoubtedly the most important cause is the immigration into the country of Gurkhas who, because of over-crowding in their own land of Nepal, find in Sikkim an ideal spot in which to settle.

This contact between the virile and enterprising Gurkhas and the easy-going and indolent Lepchas has proved disastrous to the latter who have now either been absorbed by the Gurkhas, or at least driven farther and farther into the mountains.

Always a peace-loving race, the Lepchas have been repeatedly conquered by the surrounding hill tribes, with the result that many of their old customs have vanished. Even their own rich and beautiful language is now seldom heard. With their literature destroyed by the Tibetans and their traditions forgotten, this once free and independent race are now the poorest people—the coolie class in Sikkim.

The Lepcha tribe is composed of a number of clans, but the grouping of these is a purely local and haphazard affair. Indeed, the functions of the clan are merely used for regulating marriage, because a man is not allowed to marry a girl belonging to his own clan. This is exogamy; but Lepcha exogamy is of a special kind because it does permit a man to marry a girl who is related to his father, always provided the relationship is removed by not fewer than five generations.

Their villages consist merely of scattered houses. These are raised six feet off the ground (for the local rainfall is heavy) and the siting of any new house is effected by a ceremony of divination. The Lepchas have no furniture beyond a cooking-pot. For clothes the men wear shorts and cotton shirts, the women an unattractive one-piece garment.

In appearance the Lepchas have sallow, Mongolian features and matted black hair. They are honest, indolent, cheerful, not thrifty, and very dirty. They have no interest in the outside world and it is reported that most of the people were quite unaware of the two World Wars.

There are no leaders in the villages, but a *Mandal* or headman is appointed by the government. His sole duty is to collect taxes. Being illiterate this man carries the whole of his file information in his head. Each house has to pay tax and this is levied by each individual living there having to do three days' labour for the public benefit.

Sikkim is profuse in vegetation of all kinds. There are over 4,000 species of flowering plants, 200 species of ferns and 400 species of orchids to be found in the country—a plant-collectors paradise. No other country in the world can present such variety, for the climate ranges from the tropical to the polar. Here also 600 kinds of butterflies, 2,000 kinds of moths and 600 species of birds have been identified. The Lepchas are wonderful woodmen, knowing, like so many primitive tribes, the ways of beasts and birds, and possessing an extensive zoological and botanical nomenclature of their own.

But drink and sex are the only real recreations of this vanishing tribe. Their essential wants are so easily met that they have considerable time on their hands to indulge in debasing habits. Sexual promiscuity is carried to such excess, from the earliest years, that it results in a total absence of jealousy. It is evidently realized that under such conditions the people could not live in harmony and life would become intolerable if sexual jealousy were to obtain.

The absence of possession and individual devotion is a

state of mind that it is difficult for us to comprehend. There are few people who would deny that being in love is the most exalted of human emotions. Yet, with the Lepchas there can be no question of love. Among them there is no question of adultery or even incest. Their method of classifying relationships, too, is so elastic that the most distant cousins rank as brothers and sisters, and between all these marriages are arranged or sexual relationships quite freely permitted.

It is easy to disapprove of the habits of primitive peoples. Nevertheless, since our society has grown so complicated it is in the examination of primitive peoples that we can solve some of our own urgent social problems. John Morris, an anthropologist who spent some months living among the Lepchas, found, for instance, that most so-called primitive societies, like the Lepchas, live relatively simple and un-complicated lives; and by confining ourselves to a small and self-contained community it is still possible to watch the behaviour of the individual in the group and, on the other hand, to see what effect the group has on the individual. "Which of us," he asks, "is the happier?"